TESTE DEIN WISSEN

Wie gut bin ich in

ENGLISCH

Grundwortschatz

Heike Mensch

Compact Verlag

Redaktion: Burkhard Engelmann, Heike Mensch
Umschlaggestaltung: Inga Koch
Printed in Germany
ISBN: 3-8174-7203-X
7272031

Inhalt

Abkürzungsverzeichnis

UK	=	Britisches Englisch
US	=	Amerikanisches Englisch
Q	=	Question/Frage
A	=	Answer/Antwort

Vorwort

Dieses Übungsbuch behandelt die wichtigsten Bereiche des englischen Wortschatzes. Mit den 333 abwechslungsreichen und spielerischen Übungen können Sie Ihren Wortschatz testen und erweitern.

Das Buch ist nach Wortfeldern gegliedert. Am Anfang finden Sie Übungen zu Begriffen aus den wichtigsten Bereichen des täglichen Lebens und zu Wörtern, die Sie im Ausland oder in der Konversation mit englischsprachigen Besuchern und Besucherinnen immer wieder benötigen werden.

Weiterhin bietet das Buch Ihnen die Möglichkeit, sich den Grundwortschatz zu Ihren speziellen Interessengebieten gezielt anzueignen. Ob Sie sich über Politik, Ihren Beruf oder Sport austauschen möchten, nach dem Erarbeiten der entsprechenden Kapitel wird Ihnen jedes Gespräch in der englischen Sprache mehr Spaß machen.

Mit dem Lösungsteil im Anhang können Sie Ihre Antworten auf Richtigkeit überprüfen. Wichtige Fragen zum Gebrauch bestimmter Wörter werden in Merkkästen gesondert erklärt.

Alle Übungen sind so konzipiert, daß sie ohne zusätzliche Materialien gelöst werden können. Sie benötigen nur einen Kugelschreiber oder Bleistift, um die Fragen und Worträtsel in diesem Buch zu beantworten.

Viel Erfolg!

Introductions / Sich vorstellen

Find the 9 mistakes that are hidden in this text. / Suchen Sie die 9 Fehler, die sich im Text versteckt haben. **1**

Hello. I am your new vocabulary trainer. I am still quiete young and you are one for my first readers.

I was born in the year 1996 into a large and good-known family of educational books. My ancestors are successful dictionaries, grammar books and works of reference. Our place for birth is the city of Munich. However, you can meat us in very much places on Europe and sometimes on other continents.

I am pleased to have meat you and I am looking toward working with you.

Which word does not fit? / Welches Wort paßt nicht? **2**

a) Hello! Good morning! How do you do? Good Luck!

b) Farewell, Good Bye, yours affectionately, cheerio, so long.

Connect the form of address to the person. / Verbinden Sie die Anrede mit der Person. **3**

A president	Hi, Honey!
A good friend	Hello, Love!
The Pope	Good morning, Madam/Sir.
Your husband	Good evening, Your Holiness.
Your baby daughter	Good morning, Madam/Sir.
A queen	There you are, old chum!
Your boss	Good evening, Your Highness.

Fill in the right word. / Fügen Sie das passende Wort ein. **4**

a) Do you remember what her sister´s ______________ is? (name, call)

b) I´m not quite ______________, but I think it is Paula. (right, sure)

c) You look ______________. Have we met before? (familiar, known)

d) I believe not. I do not ______________ you. (realise, recognise)

5 **Which sentence is correct? / Welcher Satz stimmt?**

a) You remember me of the actress from the movie „Dr. Zhivago“. ☒

b) You remind me of the actress from the movie „Dr. Zhivago“. ☐

c) You recognise me of the actress from the movie „Dr. Zhivago“. ☐

0

6 **Fill in the correct interrogative pronoun. / Fügen Sie das passende Fragewort ein.**

a) ________ is your name?

b) ________ were you born?

c) ________ are your parents?

d) ________ are you planning to arrive?

7 **Fill in the gaps. / Ergänzen Sie die Lücken im Text.**

is introduce noticed met living is know

Hallo, Karen. May I ____________ you to my husband Frank? I don't think the two of you have ____________ before. Frank, this ____________ my old friend Karen. Karen, this ____________ Frank.

Frank and I first ____________ at my brother's birthday party even though we had been ____________ in the same street for two years. We did not ____________ that we were almost neighbours.

8 **Connect the halves. / Verbinden Sie folgende Satzhälften.**

How do	you today?
I am pleased	meet again soon!
It was lovely	to meet you.
I hope we will	seeing you again.
How are	you do?

9 **Explain the meaning of the following idioms in other words. / Erklären Sie folgende Sprichwörter auf englisch.**

a) to call on somebody

____

b) to call somebody names

____

c) to meet someone half way

____

d) to meet with misfortune

____

Specify the location. / Ergänzen Sie die Ortsangaben. 10

_______, right here, is my colleague Edna. Standing _______ to her is her boyfriend Sven. The woman _______, not in front of the little table, is my sister Andrea and the couple sitting _______ the couch are my parents.

How are you feeling? Connect the English and German pairs. / Verbinden Sie die englischen mit den deutschen Auskünften. 11

Fine, thanks.	Es geht so.
So-so.	Miserabel.
Can't complain.	Gut, danke.
Very well, thank you.	Sehr gut, danke!
Down in the dumps.	Kann nicht klagen.

Complete the sentences in English. / Ergänzen Sie die Sätze auf englisch. 12

a) I've come to say ___________. (sich verabschieden)
b) What time are you ___________? (weggehen/-fahren)
c) My train ___________ at 6 p.m. (abfahren)
d) I have ___________ a taxi for 5.30 p.m. (bestellt)

Which sentence is correct? / Welcher Satz stimmt? 13

a) Please, give my greetings to your mother. ☐
b) Please, give my regards to your mother. ☐
c) Please, say regards to your mother from me. ☐

14 **Match the answers to the questions or statements. / Verbinden Sie die Antworten mit den Fragen oder Aussagen.**

Would you like to have a drink with me?	– Thank you, I also enjoyed our conversation.
It's been lovely talking to you.	– Yes, I would very much like to.
Shall we meet tomorrow evening?	– I would rather not see you again.
Would you like to go to a pub?	– I'm sorry, I can't. I'm busy tomorrow.
When can we meet again?	– I would prefer to go to a café.

Family and Friends / Familie und Freunde

15 **Who is who? / Wer ist was?**

a) My sister's son is my ____________.

b) My brother's father is my ____________.

c) My mother's father is my ____________.

d) My aunt's daughter is my ____________.

e) My daughter's daughter is my ____________.

16 **Which ten members of the family are hidden here? / Welche zehn Familienmitglieder haben sich hier versteckt?**

g	e	f	a	n	e	p	h	e	w	l
k	r	f	i	a	g	l	o	b	s	t
o	d	a	u	g	h	t	e	r	d	c
n	i	t	n	o	s	h	a	k	i	h
u	n	h	i	d	y	i	p	o	s	i
n	d	e	g	g	m	s	s	t	i	l
c	a	r	o	d	o	o	n	t	t	d
l	i	v	e	a	u	n	t	e	e	y
e	s	r	s	d	n	s	a	h	p	r
n	y	u	p	d	f	g	t	k	e	b
m	o	m	m	y	j	o	n	n	y	r

Complete the sentences. / Ergänzen Sie folgende Sätze. 17

a) When my mother remarried, I found it hard to get on with my new ______ at first.

b) This man's daughter, my ______ , later became my best friend.

c) My mother had a son with her second husband. This child is my ______ .

d) My new father now is my grandmother's favourite ______ .

Which word does not fit? / Welches Wort paßt nicht? 18

a) parents, grandchild, daughter, home, father.

b) marriage, independence day, baptism, engagement, family reunion.

c) brother, grandfather, nephew, cousin, uncle, daddy.

Fill in the gaps. / Ergänzen Sie die Lücken. 19

in-laws *lineage* *family reunion* *family seat* *ancestors*

Every two years all the members of our family gather for a ___________ .
My parents, my brothers and sisters, and all my cousins come. Some of our common ___________ come from the 18th century.
All the relatives not related by blood are my ___________ .
At the reunions we enjoy talking about our long ___________ . We all descend from a large farm, our original ___________ in the Black Forest.

Some words in these sentences are wrong. Correct them. / Berichtigen Sie die falschen Wörter in diesen Sätzen. 20

a) Peter's husband has just given birth to twins.

b) I like Judith very much. She is my best enemy.

c) My sister is 6 years old, my brother 9, I am 12. I am the youngest.

d) Tom looking forward to his 18th birthday when he will be an adolescent.

What are they like? Fill in the gaps. / Ergänzen Sie die Lücken. 21

nail *post* *horse* *bat* *picture*

a) My great-aunt has difficulty hearing. She is as deaf as a ___________ .

b) Her old poodle isn't much better off. He is as blind as a ___________ .

c) That muscular actor is as strong as a ___________ .

d) He always plays the role of policemen who are as hard as ___________s.

e) Those attractive children are as pretty as a ___________ .

Jobs and Professions / Arbeit und Beruf

22 **What was their occupation? / Was waren sie von Beruf?**

Paul Bocuse	________________
Marlene Dietrich	________________
Indira Ghandi	________________
John Lennon	________________
Sherlock Holmes	________________
Vincent van Gogh	________________
Confucius	________________
Franz Beckenbauer	________________
Madame Curie	________________
Maria Callas	________________

23 **On the job. Fill in the correct term. / Finden Sie den passenden Ausdruck.**

staff retiree freelance daily duties profession jobs civil servant

a) I am not employed by any newspaper. I work as a _________ reporter.

b) Klaus is a doctor. He is in the medical _________ .

c) This is a small company. It has a _________ of only 14 people.

d) The student has held many _________ . She has worked as a tour guide, a bar keeper and as an interpreter.

e) When he turned 65 my father stopped working. Now, he is a _________ .

f) Ulrike is employed by the state. She is a _________ .

g) My _________ include checking the mail, reading the papers and writing reports.

24 **Find the female form. / Ergänzen Sie die weibliche Form.**

actor	________________
monk	________________

tailor ____________________

sales clerk ____________________

headmaster ____________________

waiter ____________________

policeman ____________________

priest ____________________

poet ____________________

emperor ____________________

Match the words with their definitions. / Verbinden Sie die Begriffe mit ihren Definitionen. 25

a) job	– a physical or mental activity that requires much effort
b) profession	– a specific duty
c) labour	– requires special knowledge and often academic training
d) occupation	– a physical or mental activity
e) work	– the principal business of one's life

Which definition does not explain the word *occupation*? / Welche Definition von *occupation* ist falsch? 26

a) an activity in which one is engaged ☐
b) the principal business of one's life ☐
c) a responsible position at one's workplace ☐
d) the control of an area by a foreign army ☐

Fill in the gaps. / Ergänzen Sie die Lücken. 27

composer inventor discoverer creator

a) Christopher Columbus was one of the greatest ________ s that ever lived.
b) Johann Sebastian Bach is the ________ of many well-known organ pieces.
c) Alexander Graham Bell was the ________ of the telephone.
d) The ________ of the „Mona Lisa" is Leonardo da Vinci.

28 **Fill in the right idiom with *work*. / Ergänzen Sie die idiomatischen Ausdrücke mit *work*.**

worked off *worked out* *worked* *worked up*

a) We tried many different methods, but only one ___________.

b) Every evening she ___________ her anger at the gym.

c) The volume of a sphere can be ___________ if you know the formula.

d) They had ___________ a clever scheme to rob a bank.

e) He was all ___________ after he had lost his wallet.

29 **Name the occupation with the right form of *a/an*. / Nennen Sie den Beruf mit der richtigen Form des Artikels *a/an*.**

a) The person who repairs a broken stove is ____ ___________ .

b) The person who decides if a thief is guilty is ____ ___________ .

c) The person who gives blessings in church is ____ ___________ .

d) The person who cures you if you are ill is ____ ___________ .

e) The person who puts out a fire is ____ ___________ .

f) The person who fills an aching tooth is ____ ___________ .

g) The person who makes new furniture is ____ ___________ .

h) The person who writes books is ____ ___________ .

i) The person who gives you homework is ____ ___________ .

30 **Which sentence has a different meaning? / Welcher Satz hat eine andere Bedeutung?**

a) What do you do for a living? ☐

b) What is your line of work? ☐

c) How does it work? ☐

d) What is your occupation? ☐

31 **Fill in the English. / Ergänzen Sie die Sätze.**

a) Walter works in an office. He is a _______ . (Angestellter)

b) If you want to be a cook, you must learn that trade as an ____ . (Lehrling)

c) Electricians, butchers, tailors and plumbers are all ____ . (Facharbeiter)

d) Our jeweller, Mrs. White, is a very skilled _______ . (Kunsthandwerkerin)

Rank the following words in order of experience. / Ordnen Sie die Begriffe nach dem Rang oder Alter. 32

a) skilled worker, apprentice, foreman, director, manager.

b) minister of education, teacher, principal, pupil.

c) toddler, baby, senior citizen, adult, adolescent.

d) bishop, priest, archbishop, pope, acolyte.

e) empress, knight, queen, duke.

Who needs these objects? / Wer braucht diese Dinge? 33

a) thread, pins, silk, sewing machine ______________

b) wrench, bolts, oil, screw driver ______________

c) typewriter, telephone, letter opener ______________

d) rope, telescope, mast, sail ______________

e) chisel, marble, hammer, file ______________

f) flour, sieve, eggs, oven ______________

g) handcuffs, gun, siren, uniform ______________

h) accounts, currency, stocks, safes ______________

i) injection, x-ray, stethoscope ______________

j) scissors, comb, shampoo, colour ______________

Fill in the gaps. / Ergänzen Sie die Lücken. 34

salary wage pay

a) Builders can earn a good ____________.

b) The manager's ____________ was much higher than his secretary's.

c) The union decided that its members deserved higher ____________.

Which sentence is wrong? / Welcher Satz ist falsch? 35

a) I work flexitime. ☐

b) I work shifts. ☐

c) I work promotion. ☐

d) I work freelance. ☐

36 **Fill in the prepositions. / Ergänzen Sie die Präpositionen.**

a) My colleague is _______ holiday.

b) I had trouble _______ work today.

c) He works _______ the sales department.

d) I shall apply _______ a new job.

37 **Complete the sentences. / Ergänzen Sie die Sätze.**

entrepreneur headquarters union monopoly shares stock market

a) Our __________ are going up because our company is expanding.

b) Their grandfather was the __________ who founded the company.

c) One telephone company has the __________ of services in many countries.

d) Companies and investors trade at the __________ .

e) After the talks had broken down, a strike was organised by the __________ .

f) Most German banks have their __________ in Frankfurt/Main.

38 **Match the English and German idioms. / Verbinden Sie die passenden englischen und deutschen Sprichwörter.**

a) There's honour among thieves.	– Ranklotzen.
b) To be as mad as a hatter.	– Eine Meise unterm Hut haben.
c) To cut one's coat according to one's cloth.	– Ein ganz geriebener Kerl sein.
d) To put one's nose to the grindstone.	– Sich nach der Decke strecken.
e) To be a smooth customer.	– Eine Krähe hackt der anderen kein Auge aus.

At School / In der Schule

39 **Fill in the gaps. / Ergänzen Sie die Lücken.**

a) The first school that a child can go to is a __________.

b) My six year old son started __________ this year.

c) Larry is studying to be an architect at a __________.

d) That girl is a __________ at the local high school.

e) Professor Smith is a leading __________ of Roman history.

Which sentences are wrong? / Welche Sätze sind falsch? 40

a) There was not one mistake in Marion's excellent spelling test. ☐

b) There was not one flaw in Marion's excellent spelling test. ☐

c) There was not one blunder in Marion's excellent spelling test. ☐

d) There was not one fault in Marion's excellent spelling test. ☐

e) There was not one error in Marion's excellent spelling test. ☐

Fill in the gaps. / Ergänzen Sie diese Sätze. 41

a) I like mathematics, but my favourite __________ is art.

b) One needs chalk to write on a __________.

c) Our school offers many __________ activities in the afternoon, such as a school choir, a hockey team and a chess club.

d) There is a large selection of children's novels in the school __________.

e) The hall with many seats and a stage in it is the school __________.

Ten subjects are hidden in this block. Can you find them? / Welche zehn Schulfächer sind hier versteckt? 42

P	E	N	S	T	M	O	M	O	U	R
L	I	T	E	R	A	T	U	R	E	I
A	G	I	N	G	T	T	S	U	G	H
N	R	E	K	A	H	E	I	P	A	G
E	A	D	O	L	S	T	C	H	H	A
T	M	Z	U	G	D	O	L	E	I	M
E	M	O	G	E	R	S	A	P	S	E
A	A	M	P	B	E	A	T	O	T	A
S	R	I	C	R	A	T	P	L	O	T
G	Y	M	X	A	R	T	I	H	R	I
A	C	H	E	M	I	S	T	R	Y	E

43 **In which subject would you learn about the following? / In welchem Fach wird folgendes gelehrt?**

a) poems, novels, metaphors, rhyme ____________

b) The French Revolution, World War I, Cleopatra, Bismarck ____________

c) obtuse angles, squares, circumference, triangles ____________

d) droughts, rivers, oceans, the North Pole ____________

e) commas, capitalisation, word order, irregular verbs ____________

f) photosynthesis, bacteria, nerve systems, mammals ____________

44 **Fill in the opposites of the underlined words. / Ergänzen Sie das Gegenteil der unterstrichenen Wörter.**

a) If you do not get enough points to <u>pass</u> the test, you will ____________ it.

b) If you are very <u>diligent</u>, you are not ____________ .

c) If you always finish your tasks <u>swiftly</u>, you are not ____________ .

d) If your books are <u>impeccable</u>, you are not ____________ .

e) If you are always <u>on time</u>, you are never ____________ .

45 **Who is in charge of these things/groups? / Wer beaufsichtigt diese Dinge/Gruppen?**

a) information for a career choice ____________________

b) the books in the library ____________________

c) a football team ____________________

d) the school choir ____________________

e) all the teachers ____________________

46 **Fill in the missing words. / Ergänzen Sie die Lücken.**

Before school starts in the morning, all the children lock their coats and their school bags in their ____________ . When the ____________rings they hurry to their ____________ .

In some rooms the children sit at normal tables, but most classrooms have proper school ____________ .

If a teacher ____________ a tests that was written the day before, the children are very curious about everybody's ____________ .

There is a long __________ in the middle of the school day with enough time to eat a __________ and play in the __________ .
On special occasions the pupils and the teachers __________ in the auditorium before they go home and listen to the principal make __________ .

Fill in the right form of the idiom with *take*. / Ergänzen Sie den richtigen idiomatischen Ausdruck mit *take*. 47

take an engine to pieces *take no notice of* *take my grandfather back* *take up* *take turns* *take for granted* *take them all by surprise*

a) After a short break the orchestra __________ practising again.
b) In cricket the pupils __________ hitting the ball.
c) The explosion in the laboratory __________.
d) European children __________ their well equipped schools __________ .
e) The novel „Tom Sawyer“ __________ to his own youth.
f) In the workshop the children had to __________ .
g) The noisy children __________ teacher's effort to quieten them.

Which word does not fit? / Welches Wort paßt nicht? 48

a) grade, result, evaluation, completion.
b) test, demonstrate, check, examine.
c) copy, draw, sketch, paint, illustrate.
d) tidy, orderly, timid, neat, accurate.
e) inventive, creative, innovative, abstract.
f) speak, lecture, interrogate, talk, tell.

Fill in the correct prepositions. / Ergänzen Sie die Präpositionen. 49

a) Mary excelled __________ maths, her favourite subject.
b) The chemistry lab was __________ the top floor of the building.
c) There is a football match __________ our school this Saturday.
d) Neil is the best pianist __________ his entire school.
d) Unfortunately, the school bus arrived five minutes __________ school had already started.

50 **Complete the sentences. / Ergänzen Sie die Sätze.**

tutor lecturer instructor teacher

a) This morning the class was pleased because the ________ was late.

b) When Billy almost failed history his parents hired a ________.

c) The seminar on Shakespeare was taught by an experienced ________.

d) The driving ________ sighed as the learner stalled the car once again.

51 **Give one antonym for each word. / Nennen Sie ein Antonym (Gegensatz) für jedes Wort.**

a) determination ________________

b) listless ________________

c) alienate ________________

d) assist ________________

e) improve ________________

f) modesty ________________

g) moderate ________________

52 **What could it be? / Was könnte das sein?**

a) It is long and thin.
You can write with it.
It must be refilled with ink regularly. ________________

b) It is very light.
You should have one in your pencil case.
It can erase writing. ________________

c) It is completely straight.
It is usually made of wood or plastic.
One uses it to draw lines. ________________

d) It has many pages.
It is organised in alphabetical order.
You use it in language class. ________________

e) All the children of one school have it.
It is made of cloth.
It shows to which school the child goes. ________________

Which is the right definition of *courteous*? / Was ist die Bedeutung von *courteous?* 53

a) having the strength to withstand fear and danger ☐
b) of a very elegant and stylish quality ☐
c) the outermost rim of a tennis court ☐
c) marked by respect and consideration for others ☐

Complete the idioms. / Ergänzen Sie die Sprichwörter. 54

a) Tom thinks he knows everything, but he is really only __________-baked.
b) When the sisters dress alike they look like __________ peas in a pod.
c) Don't believe anything that __________-faced man says. He always tells several versions of the story.
d) After his fifth whiskey our host was __________ sheets to the wind.
e) Grandfather always lies down to have his __________ winks after lunch.
f) You will never reach Rome in that car. It is on its __________ leg.
g) When the airport was closed due to flooding, Karen exclaimed „That's the __________ straw to a ruined vacation!"

In the City / In der Stadt

Who lives where? / Wer wohnt wo? 55

a) a nun lives in ____________________
b) a king and a queen live in ____________________
c) an orphan lives in ____________________
d) a traveller lives in ____________________
e) a very old person lives in ____________________
f) a patient sometimes stays in ____________________

Fill in the right word. / Fügen Sie das passende Wort ein. 56

nearest *direction* *one-way* *area* *way*

a) I think I have lost my __________ .
b) Excuse me, could you tell me where the __________ public phone is?

c) I'm sorry, I can't. I don't know this __________ either.

d) I'll try to go back in the __________ that I came from.

e) You must take a different street because this is a __________ street.

57 **What is a *dormitory*?**

a) a shop that sells beds and mattresses

b) a very large room that can be entered from two sides

c) a place where pupils live if their home is far from school

d) the sleeping tract of a palace

58 **Arrange from smallest to biggest. / Ordnen Sie vom Kleinsten zum Größten.**

a) house, cottage, palace, mansion

b) town, hamlet, city, village

c) highway, alley, path, street

d) suite, room, building, chamber

59 **Complete the sentences. / Ergänzen Sie die Sätze.**

a) Many Christians worship in a _______ every Sunday.

b) The chimes that you hear every hour come from that high _______ .

c) Notre Dame in Paris and St. Paul's in London are two of the most famous _______ in Europe.

d) Visitors can pray or meditate in a little _______ at the cemetery.

e) The big building with the Star of David over the entrance is the ______ .

f) An imam leads the prayers at a _______ .

g) The Parthenon is one of the biggest ancient Greek _______ .

60 **What is it? / Was ist es?**

a) a person who walks in the street ____________

b) the place where two streets cross ____________

c) the black and white stripes that cross a street ____________

d) the signs that regulate traffic ____________

e) the red, yellow and green lights in the street ____________

f) a person who rides a bicycle ____________

g) a man who sells tickets on a bus ____________

h) the side of the street that is reserved for people ____________

i) a person who sells thing in the street ____________

j) the coin-operated machine that measures parking time ____________

Fill in the gaps. / Ergänzen Sie die Lücken. 61

My uncle Bernie lives in one of the many _______ that surround Chicago. There, he owns the right half of a _______ house. Before his daughter Cathy moved into the other half, she had rented a flat in a large _______ in the middle of Chicago.

Cathy finally moved out of the _______ because she felt threatened by the gangs that roamed her _______ . Now, she misses the view of the Sears Tower, the most famous _______ in Chicago - but she is glad that she can park her car right at her front door and no longer in an underground _____ .

Where do you buy the following things? / Wo können Sie folgendes kaufen? 62

a) milk, butter, cheese in a ____________

b) bread, cake, rolls in a ____________

c) meat and sausages at a ____________

d) dictionaries and books in a ____________

e) newspapers and magazines at a ____________

f) notebooks, envelopes, paper in a ____________

g) tools, nails, paint in a ____________

h) medicine, bandages at a ____________

i) ice cream in a ____________

j) necklaces, diamonds, rings at a ____________

h) aeroplane tickets, a booking at a hotel at a ____________

Fill in the gaps. / Ergänzen Sie die Sätze. 63

a) You should have no problem finding Baker Street if you look up the route in the __________ .

b) I arrived at the __________ with enough time to buy a paper before my train left.

c) The little grocery shop lost many customers after a huge __________ opened in the neighbourhood.

d) There is a good collection of expressionist paintings at our __________ .

e) Tonight's performance at the __________ will be cancelled because the star is ill.

f) The tea party took place in a dainty __________ in the garden.

g) The ducks and swans like to swim in the little __________ in the park.

64 **Fill in the prepositions. / Ergänze Sie die Präpositionen.**

a) Highway 696 cuts ________ the middle of our town.

b) Take the elevator, if you want to go ________ the top floor.

c) I live ________ the second floor of the building.

d) The theatre is right ________ to the supermarket.

e) There is a park ________ the rugby stadium.

f) His house is ________ the country.

g) I live ________ the end of the street.

h) I always go to town ________ bus.

65 **Which word does not fit? / Welches Wort paßt nicht?**

a) shed, stable, cottage, barn ☐

b) lane, alley, avenue, direction ☐

c) roam, rove, run, stray, ramble ☐

d) narrow, diminutive, miniature, tiny ☐

e) build, erect, devise, construct, put up ☐

66 **Give one antonym. / Nennen Sie jeweils ein Antonym (einen Gegensatz).**

a) delicate ________________

b) demolish ________________

c) elaborate ________________

d) primitive ________________

e) attract ______________

f) former ______________

Give the British equivalent of these American words. / Nennen Sie den britischen Begriff für diese amerikanischen Wörter. 67

an apartment ______________

the ground floor ______________

rest rooms ______________

a faucet ______________

an elevator ______________

the sidewalk ______________

a parking structure ______________

a gas station ______________

the drugstore ______________

a subway ______________

a traffic light ______________

a store ______________

Fill in the right idiom with *go*. Fügen Sie einen idiomatischen Ausdruck mit *go* ein. 68

a) Don't drink that old juice. I'm sure it has __________ (spoilt).

b) They assured me that they would come on Sunday. When they did not arrive I realised that they had __________ (to lie).

c) His success has __________ (make conceited).

d) His health __________ (deteriorate) when he broke his leg after he had the flu.

e) That shop is gone, it has __________ (stop trading).

f) The clock __________ (malfunction) after I had dropped it on the floor.

g) If there aren't enough pens to __________ (for everybody), we will get some more.

h) She __________ (repeat) what she had seen before she answered the policewoman's question.

69 **In which sentence is the usage of *domestic* wrong? / In welchen Satz wird *domestic* falsch benutzt?**

a) The Smiths are a peaceful family that enjoys domestic tranquility. ☐

b) Cows and horses are the most popular domestic animals. ☐

c) The domestic language of Australia is English. ☐

d) Every Saturday the whole family does domestic duties. ☐

e) We buy only domestic wine as we do not agree with long transport routes. ☐

At Home / Zu Hause

70 **In which room would you do the following? / In welchem Zimmer tun Sie folgendes?**

a) entertain guests ____________

b) cook food ____________

c) work after hours ____________

d) take a shower ____________

e) keep food for storage ____________

f) let the children keep their toys and play ____________

g) store old things you don't need anymore ____________

h) keep a wine collection ____________

71 **Name the parts of a building. / Nennen Sie die Teile eines Gebäudes.**

a) the highest point of a slanted roof ____________

b) it is on the roof and smoke comes out of it ____________

c) one makes a fire in it ____________

d) steps that lead to the upper storeys ____________

e) they are made of fired clay and used for building ____________

f) it projects from a wall and has a railing ____________

g) a roofed area that is attached to a building ____________

h) you close them when you go to sleep ____________

What is the name of the room intended for sleeping? / Wie heißt das Zimmer zum Schlafen? 72

a) rest room ☐
b) bed room ☐
c) sleeping room ☐
d) bedroom ☐
e) sleeproom ☐

Connect the word with its definition. / Verbinden Sie das Wort mit seiner Erklärung. 73

a) portal	a roofed entrance to a building
b) threshold	the place or the act of entry
c) entrance	a swinging or sliding barrier that closes an entry
d) gate	a grand and imposing entrance
e) door	an opening in a wall or fence
f) porch	the plank or stone that lies under a door

What device do you need to do the following? / Was brauchen Sie, um folgendes zu tun? 74

a) to eat soup ____________
b) to cut bread ____________
c) to beat cream ____________
d) to cover a mattress ____________
e) to cover a window ____________
f) to sweep the floor ____________
g) to keep clothes in ____________
h) to open a bottle of wine ____________
i) to open a bottle of beer ____________
j) to open a tin/a can ____________
k) to light a cigarette ____________

Which sentences are correct? / Welche Sätze sind richtig? 75

a) Joe's house was not harmed by the tornado. ☐

b) Joe's house was not hurt by the tornado. ☐
c) Joe's house was not damaged by the tornado. ☐
d) Joe's house was not injured by the tornado. ☐

76 **Complete the pairs. / Ergänzen Sie die Paare.**

cups and ____________
knives and ____________
salt and ____________
pillow and ____________
tables and ____________
shoes and ____________
plug and ____________

77 **Translate these household activities. / Übersetzen Sie folgende Tätigkeiten im Haushalt.**

a) Wäsche waschen ____________
b) Geschirr spülen ____________
c) Geschirr abtrocknen ____________
d) Vorhänge zumachen ____________
e) Licht anmachen ____________
f) fernsehschauen ____________
g) etwas leiser stellen ____________
h) Telefon beantworten ____________
i) Kaffee kochen ____________
j) eine Kerze anzünden ____________
k) eine Kerze ausmachen ____________

78 **What are the collective nouns for these things? / Was ist der Sammelbegriff für diese Dinge?**

a) pillow cases, sheets, blankets ____________
b) tables, chairs, bookshelves ____________
c) knives, forks, spoons ____________
d) screwdriver, hammer, wrench ____________

Fill in the gaps. / Ergänzen Sie die Sätze. 79

a) Her rich aunt has covered the walls of her house with silken __________ .

b) The kitchen went dark after the __________ had blown.

c) In winter Hillary sleeps under an __________ filled with feathers.

d) Do the dishes by hand in the kitchen __________ .

e) All electrical appliances get their current from a wall __________ .

Name the type of seat. / Benennen Sie die Sitzgelegenheit. 80

a) a chair for a baby __________________

b) a settee for two people __________________

c) a long seat for two or more people __________________

d) a very comfortable, upholstered chair __________________

e) a long, upholstered seat __________________

f) a chair that moves to and fro __________________

g) a folding chair for the garden __________________

h) the chair of a king or queen __________________

Fill in *still*, *yet* or *already*. / Ergänzen Sie die Sätze mit *still*, *yet* oder *already*. 81

a) Don't buy any milk. I have ___________ bought some.

b) I have been thinking all day and I am ___________ confused.

c) The postman has not come ___________ .

d) Not another vase! I have ___________ received six vases this Christmas.

e) Pete ___________ lives in the same house in which he was born.

f) Have you finished painting Bill's portrait ___________ ?

Fill in the right word. / Fügen Sie das richtige Wort ein. 82

home residence dwellings house

a) After they married Steve and Becky bought a new ___________ .

b) Becky redecorated it and made it into a lovely ___________ .

c) The company built ___________ for 30 people.

d) Lord Chatterly's ___________ was a 60-room mansion.

83 **Which word does not fit? / Welches Wort paßt nicht?**

a) landlady, tenant, rent, wage

b) border, edge, line, boundary

c) remunerate, produce, pay, remit

d) pointed, lofty, tall, soaring

84 **Fill in the gaps. / Ergänzen Sie die Sätze.**

a) The person who leases a flat is a __________ .

b) The price one must pay for a flat every month is the __________ .

c) The private road that leads to the garage is the __________ .

d) The barrier at the boundary of the garden is the __________ .

85 **Name the household appliance. / Wie heißt das Haushaltsgerät?**

a) it toasts bread __________

b) it makes coffee __________

c) you dry your hair with it __________

d) it washes dishes __________

e) it washes clothes __________

f) it dries clothes __________

g) it cleans the carpet __________

h) it cuts the grass __________

86 **Which sentence is right? / Welcher Satz ist richtig?**

a) Alan does a shower every morning. ☐

b) Alan takes a shower every morning. ☐

c) Alan showers every morning. ☐

d) Alan takes a showering every morning. ☐

87 **Fill in the gaps. / Ergänzen Sie die Lücken.**

plumbing fixtures bath(tub) basins shower pipes tiles mirror

James and Sally spent many hours redecorating their bathroom. They had to lay new __________ because they changed the position of the __________ . They put new __________ on the walls and installed two

__________ because they want to get ready at the same time every morning. They covered the wall above the basins with a large __________ made of Italian glass.
Since both like to relax in hot water after work, they chose an especially comfortable __________ , but they also built in a __________ for quick refreshing in the morning.

Translate the following. / Übersetzen Sie die Tätigkeiten. 88

duschen ________________
baden ________________
Zähne putzen ________________
sich schminken ________________
Haare kämmen ________________
Füße schrubben ________________
Nägel schneiden ________________
Haare föhnen ________________
Schnürsenkel zubinden ________________
Mantel zuknöpfen ________________
Mantel aufknöpfen ________________

Fill in the prepositions. / Ergänzen Sie die Präpositionen. 89

a) The guests knocked _______ the door.
b) We hung (up) pictures _______ the walls.
c) I jumped out _______ bed this morning.
d) The baby is sleeping _______ the cradle.
e) The honeypot is sticking _______ the table.
f) Put the ashtray _______ the shelf.
g) The glass fell _______ the table and broke.
h) The wine spilt _______ the floor.
i) Uta has many books _______ her bookshelf.

90 **Connect the English and German idioms. / Verbinden Sie die englischen mit den entsprechenden deutschen Sprichwörtern.**

To pull the wool over somebody's eyes.	Sein/Ihr wahres Gesicht zeigen.
To take somebody for a ride.	Eine Hand im Spiel haben.
To have a finger in the pie.	Jemand übers Ohr hauen.
To show one's true colours.	Jemandem Sand in die Augen streuen.
To win hands down.	Mit allen Wassern gewaschen sein.
To be up to every trick.	Mit links gewinnen.

91 **Fill in *good* or *well*. / Fügen Sie *good* oder *well ein*.**

a) Heather cooked a __________ dinner.

b) Matthew plays the piano __________ .

c) Laura is a __________ hostess.

d) Mash those potatoes __________ !

e) Jenny decorated the table __________ .

Food, Clothing, Shopping / Lebensmittel, Kleidung, Einkaufen

92 **What are these meals called? / Wie heißen diese Mahlzeiten?**

a) The first meal of the day __________

b) What you take to work to eat __________

c) You eat it at noon __________

d) In England one has it at 4 p.m. __________

e) The whole family meets for it every evening __________

f) It is a formal meal in the evening __________

g) You have it on a blanket in a park __________

Translate the following. / Übersetzen Sie folgende Sätze. 93

a) Ich habe Durst. ______________________

b) Ich lösche meinen Durst. ______________________

c) Sie haben Hunger. ______________________

d) Sie stillen ihren Hunger. ______________________

e) Sie verhungern. ______________________

f) Sie nimmt einen Imbiß ein. ______________________

g) Das ist ihre Leibspeise. ______________________

Connect the halves. / Verbinden Sie die Satzteile. 94

a) Please set	served in five minutes.
b) Dinner is	you with the dishes.
c) Do you take	for some more wine?
d) Would you care	the table for supper.
e) You can clear	milk or sugar in your tea?
f) Let me help	the table when we're done.

Choose the right word. / Wählen Sie das richtige Wort. 95

a) Tracy's parents ________ at ________ o'clock every evening. (ate, eight)

b) If you ________ vegetarians, never offer them ________ . (meat, meet)

c) After travelling in the ________ , the tourists chose a cold ________ . (dessert, desert)

d) There was no ________ in the class until each child had a ________ of cake. (peace, piece)

e) The secret ________ of the truffles in his ________ was somewhere in France. (source, sauce)

f) One ________ cheese weighs very little because there are many ________s in it. (hole, whole)

g) You need a ___________ of ________s and three apples for this cake. (pair, pear)

h) Terrence could not ________ to loose five pounds of ________ . (weight, wait)

96 **Match each food with a suitable adjective. / Verbinden Sie jede Speise mit einem passenden Adjektiv.**

champagne	fruity
french fries	bubbly
ice cream	strong
chocolate icing	rare
pickles	sweet
chilli peppers	greasy
apple pie	hot
marshmallow	soft
coffee	cold
steak	sour

97 **Name four fruit that end in *-berry*. / Nennen Sie vier Früchte, die auf *-berry* enden.**

________________ ________________

________________ ________________

98 **What is it called? / Wie heißt es?**

a) You use it instead of sugar if you are on a diet. ____________

b) It is the yellow part of an egg. ____________

c) The different foods you need to bake a cake are the ____________ .

d) All bubbly soft drinks are ____________ .

e) Beer is made at a ____________ .

f) They are the additives that make food last. ____________

g) You cut bread or roast into ____________ .

h) It makes you cry when you cut it. ____________

99 **Which word does not fit? / Welches Wort paßt nicht?**

a) cucumber, tomato, lettuce, grape, beetroot

b) onion, peach, tangerine, plum, pear

c) basil, thyme, nut, rosemary, parsley

d) fry, poach, bake, scramble, sunny-side-up

What do you call the meat of these animals? / Wie heißt das Fleisch dieser Tiere? 100

a) chicken, turkeys, ducks ________________

b) cows ________________

c) calves ________________

d) sheep ________________

e) pigs ________________

f) deer ________________

Connect the halves. / Verbinden Sie die Satzhälften. 101

a) to season	eggs
b) to fold	a steak
c) to whip	with salt and pepper
d) to fry	in egg white
e) to scramble	cream

Put the interchanged words in the right place. / Setzen Sie die vertauschten Wörter richtig ein. 102

Barbara is very choosy about her **flour**. That is why she bakes her own bread. She uses only whole wheat **spread** and other healthy **nutrition** for the dough. While the bread bakes in the oven a delicious **ingredients** permeates the whole house.

It is a fine delicacy if you **slice** some butter on a fresh **smell** of Barbara's bread.

Fill in the right idiom with *make*. / Setzen Sie den richtigen Begriff mit *make* ein. 103

make no secret of *made things worse* *make the most of* *made peace* *make out* *make a stand*

a) I can't ________ (understand) what you are saying if you whisper.

b) __________ (resist) for yourself and don't obey your brother all the time.

c) I ________ (don't conceal) my loathing for garlic.

d) ________ (exploit) your youth and go out every evening.

e) After three years of hostilities the brothers finally ________ (ended hostilities).

f) The freezing rain ________ (worsened conditions) on the roads.

104 **Which sentences are correct? / Welche Sätze sind richtig?**

a) Peter's chocolate cake tastes very good. ☐

b) Peter's chocolate cake tastes very well. ☐

c) A cup of hot tea would feel good now. ☐

d) A cup of hot tea would feel well now. ☐

e) Philip's writing has become well. ☐

f) Philip's writing has become good. ☐

105 **Fill in the English. / Setzen Sie das englische Wort ein.**

a) I've ____________ (bestellen) a table under the name of Smith.

b) Are you ready to ____________ (bestellen)?

c) We have not ____________ (entscheiden) yet.

d) I would ____________ (empfehlen) the duck.

e) May I ____________ (aufnehmen) your order now?

f) I'm sorry, we ____________ (ausgegangen sein) peas.

g) I'll ____________ (nehmen) the fish.

h) Did you ____________ (genießen) your meal?

106 **Unjumble these words needed in a restaurant. / Entwirren Sie diese Worte, die im Restaurant benötigt werden.**

a) koongbi __________________

b) nemu __________________

c) resstwai __________________

d) dorer __________________

e) tifriape __________________

f) ageverbe __________________

g) naim source __________________

What could the questions to these answers be? / Welche Fragen passen zu diesen Antworten? 107

a) Q: ______________________________________?

A: I would like some cheddar cheese, please.

b) Q: We're sold out of cheddar . ______________________?

A: Yes, I will have some gouda.

c) Q: ______________________________________?

A: That's five pound ten, altogether.

What is it? / Was ist das? 108

a) a passage between the shelves in a supermarket ______________
b) the machine that shows the amount due ______________
c) the big basket with wheels for use in a shop ______________
d) the money returned when paying ______________
e) a reduction from a regular price ______________
f) the machine that weighs goods ______________
g) the large sale at the end of the season ______________

Give the antonym of these words. / Nennen Sie das Antonym dieser Begriffe. 109

a) cheap ______________
b) heavy ______________
c) fresh ______________
d) separate ______________
e) tight ______________
f) larger ______________
g) wide ______________
h) modern ______________

Fill in a suitable word. / Setzen Sie ein passendes Wort ein. 110

a) That coat __________ (looks good on) you.
b) This colour is not __________ (favourable) to you.
c) The length must be __________ (changed).

d) This material may only be ___________ ___________ (chemically cleaned).

e) You can ____________ the shirt (change the colour) red.

f) The new tie ____________ (looks good with) his jacket.

111 Name the article of clothing. / Benennen Sie das Kleidungsstück.

a) You wear them on your hands ____________________

b) You wear them inside your shoes ____________________

c) You wear it around your neck in winter ____________________

d) You wear it around your waist to keep pants up ____________________

e) You wear it when you go swimming ____________________

f) They are big and warm shoes ____________________

g) Only women wear them on their legs ____________________

h) It is a dress to be worn under a dress ____________________

i) A jacket with a matching pair of trousers ____________________

j) It has a brim ____________________

k) Men wear it around their necks ____________________

l) It protects your clothes in the kitchen ____________________

112 Which word does not fit? / Welches Wort paßt nicht?

a) hat, cap, bowler, cape, beret

b) belt, bra, skirt, stockings, dress

c) shorts, hood, slacks, trousers, pants

d) sleeve, collar, tie, button, cuff

e) fashion, dress, frock, gown

f) bathing suit, bikini, swimming trunks, robe

g) slippers, heels, pumps, galoshes, boots

113 Fill in the gaps. / Ergänzen Sie die Sätze.

larger cut size

a) This dress does not fit. Do you have it in a different ____________ (Größe)?

b) Corpulent people are advised to wear clothes with a loose ____________ (Schnitt).

c) This shirt is too small for you. You need a ____________ one.

Which sentence is correct? / Welcher Satz ist richtig? 114

a) The princess wears her clothes five times a day. ☐

b) The princess dresses her clothes five times a day. ☐

c) The princess changes her clothes five times a day. ☐

d) The princess gets on her clothes five times a day. ☐

Some words are mixed up. Put them in the right place. / Manche Wörter sind vertauscht. Setzen Sie diese richtig ein. 115

a) Tom opened his *handkerchief* when it started to rain.

b) Grandmother's *necklace* slipped off her nose when she fell asleep.

c) Irene wiped her nose with a *umbrella*.

d) Yvonne put on a woolen *glasses* when she was cold.

e) Emily put the golden *sweater* in her jewelry box.

Find the twelve clothes/parts of clothes hidden here. / Welche zwölf Bekleidungsstücke sind hier versteckt? 116

e	p	y	j	a	m	a	s	t	a	c
l	o	e	d	i	p	e	e	h	o	a
b	e	l	t	s	i	a	k	h	n	r
l	o	v	e	t	m	t	n	a	a	d
a	r	i	t	o	i	p	u	t	x	i
z	i	p	r	c	e	c	l	l	s	g
e	a	r	s	k	n	o	o	h	p	a
r	e	s	k	i	r	t	l	a	g	n
o	v	e	r	n	n	e	i	n	t	t
e	n	d	z	g	l	o	v	e	s	a
v	e	i	l	s	f	o	x	b	o	u

Fill in the gaps. / Ergänzen Sie diese Sätze. 117

clothing clothes dress attire

a) He came to the rock concert wearing evening __________ .

b) Although he had lots of __________ , he never knew what to wear.

c) In winter people wear warm ___________ .

d) The Duchess's ___________ for the evening was highly elegant.

118 **For which word does *a pair* mean two identical items? / Bei welchem Wort bedeuted *pair* zwei gleiche Einzelstücke?**

a) a pair of boots ☐

b) a pair of trousers ☐

c) a pair of glasses ☐

d) a pair of bras ☐

119 **Which sentence has a different meaning?**

a) He was looking for a suitable pair of shoes for the wedding. ☐

b) He was looking for a fitting pair of shoes for the wedding. ☐

c) He was looking for a correct pair of shoes for the wedding. ☐

d) He was looking for an appropriate pair of shoes for the wedding. ☐

120 **Which sentence is wrong? / Welcher Satz ist falsch?**

a) Michael must shine his evening shoes before the ball. ☐

b) Michael must clear his evening shoes before the ball. ☐

c) Michael must clean his evening shoes before the ball. ☐

d) Michael must polish his evening shoes before the ball. ☐

121 **Choose the right word. / Wählen Sie das richtige Wort aus.**

a) Why do you always wear/carry that ugly hat?

b) He has warn/worn the same socks for a month!

c) Your waist/waste is too small for that belt.

d) Tim bought the shirt cheaply on sail/sale.

e) Karen cannot walk in such high heels/heals.

122 **Fill in the right form of *to dress*. / Setzen Sie die richtige Form von *to dress* ein.**

dress *dressed up* *undressed* *dress* *got dressed*

a) His little son can get ____________ by himself at bedtime.

b) Sascha ___________ as Dracula at Halloween.

c) Walter forgot to put on socks when he ___________ this morning.

d) Fiona loves to ___________ in wide, flowing skirts.

e) Guests are expected to ___________ formally for dinner.

Fill in the idioms with *run*. / Fügen Sie einen idiomatischen Ausdruck mit *run* ein. 123

a) His son ___________ (had a fever).

b) The teacher ___________ (reviewed) the most important facts.

c) I ___________ (met by chance) an old friend in town.

d) They ___________ (had much trouble) trying to import a crocodile.

e) Peter ___________ (had no more) flour when he wanted to bake a cake.

f) It is already December 23rd and ___________ (not much time left) to buy Christmas presents.

g) The murderer was ___________ (free) for three days before the police caught him.

h) A freight ship ___________ (got stuck in the ground) in the Mississippi.

Time and Holidays / Zeitangaben, Festtage und Ferien

When does it happen? / Wann geschieht es? 124

a) A new day begins at ________________.

b) February has 29 days in a ________________.

c) The sun is at its highest point at ________________.

d) The birds start to sing at ________________.

e) Owls can see best by ________________.

f) You are reading this sentence at ________________.

125 **Fill in the gaps. / Ergänzen Sie die Sätze.**

a) There are four ___________ in the year.

b) A new ___________ begins every 100 years.

c) A ___________ tells you what date it is.

d) Jeremy's ___________ wakes him up at six o'clock every morning.

e) Most people do not work on public ___________ .

f) The artist's oeuvre can be divided into four ___________ .

g) We are living in the ___________ of the computer.

126 **Which sentence is right? / Welcher Satz ist richtig?**

a) There is a full moon each 28 days. ☐

b) There is a full moon every 28 days. ☐

c) There is a full moon all 28 days. ☐

d) There is a full moon too 28 days. ☐

127 **Translate the following. / Übersetzen Sie Folgendes.**

a) aktuell ___________.

b) kürzlich ___________.

c) früher ___________.

d) in der Zukunft ___________.

e) die Nachwelt ___________.

f) gegenwärtig ___________.

g) jetzt ___________.

128 **Complete the questions. / Vervollständigen Sie die Fragen.**

a) Q: What is ___________ ?

A: It is six o'clock.

b) Q: What is ___________, please?

A: It is the seventh of March.

c) Q: And which ___________ is it?

A: It is Friday.

d) Q: Do ___________ ?

A: I'm not sure, but I think it is the sixth of March.

Which season is it? / Welche Jahreszeit ist gemeint? 129

a) It is the coldest season of the year. ____________________

b) The leaves turn red and gold in it. ____________________

c) It is the hottest season of the year. ____________________

d) The tulips bloom in this season. ____________________

e) In North America the warmest days of fall are called ____________ .

Fill in the gaps. / Ergänzen Sie die Sätze. 130

goes off *fast* *slow*

a) If your clocks are __________, you will always be late.

b) Fred thought that it was ten minutes earlier because his watch was __________.

c) Helen wakes up with a start when her alarm __________ in the morning.

Write out the time in words. / Schreiben Sie die Uhrzeit in Worten. 131

a) 9:15 a.m. ____________________

b) 4:30 p.m. ____________________

c) 12:05 p.m. ____________________

d) 8:00 p.m. ____________________

e) 11:45 a.m. ____________________

f) 7:50 p.m. ____________________

g) 5:59 p.m. ____________________

h) 10:02 a.m. ____________________

i) 11:36 p.m. ____________________

Which is not a definition of *present*? / Was ist keine Definition von *present*? 132

a) to show ☐

b) to make a gift ☐

c) to aim a weapon ☐

d) the current time ☐

e) an artistic likeness or image ☐

f) a gift ☐

133 **Fill in the gaps. / Ergänzen Sie die Lücken.**

a) year, ________, century, millennium
b) January, February, ________, April, May
c) day, week, ________, year
d) morning, midday, ________, evening, night
e) every minute, ________, daily, weekly, monthly
f) first, ________, third, fourth, fifth
g) ninth, tenth, ________, ________, thirteenth, fourteenth
h) Sunday, Monday, ________, ________, Thursday

134 **Which word does not rhyme? / Welches Wort reimt nicht?**

a) hour, power, sour, lower
b) late, eight, state, gait, freight, trite, great
c) tonight, quiet, trite, slight, quite, delight
d) slow, foe, grow, vow, follow, toe
e) among, strung, boomerang, tongue, clung
f) moon, spoon, rune, alone

135 **Fill in the English. / Ergänzen Sie die Sätze auf englisch.**

a) All the trains were ________ (verzögert) due to a strike.
b) There is an ________ (Pause) in the middle of the show.
c) The ________ (stetig) ticking of the clock lulled him to sleep.
d) A ________ (plötzlich) crash of thunder woke him up.
e) The headache pill gave only ________ (zeitweilig) relief.
f) We expect a stock market crash in the ________ (unmittelbar) future.
g) I can't understand either of you if you speak ________ (gleichzeitig).

136 **Connect each idiom with its meaning. / Verbinden Sie die idiomatischen Begriffe mit ihrer Bedeutung.**

a) ahead of time	seit jeher
b) before one's time	sehr unter Zeitdruck stehen
c) Once upon a time	früher als erwartet
d) to be pressed for time	im Wettlauf mit der Zeit

e) to race against the time — immer wieder
f) time after time — Es war einmal
g) time out of mind — bevor jemand geboren wurde

Which sentence is right? / Welcher Satz ist richtig? 137

a) Their friendship persisted just one year. ☐
b) Their friendship took just one year. ☐
c) Their friendship lasted just one year. ☐
d) Their friendship continued just one year. ☐

Name the holidays or festivals. / Nennen Sie den Festtag. 138

a) A bunny brings coloured eggs at ___________.
b) The old year ends at ___________.
c) The new year starts on ___________.
d) A country celebrates its birthday on its ___________.
e) Christians celebrate the birth of Jesus at ___________.
f) Lovers give each other presents on this day in February: ___________.
g) The day a couple was married is their ___________.
h) Children dress up as goblins and decorate pumpkins at ___________.
i) In remembrance of the Irish patron saint everybody wears green clothes on ___________.

Which sentence is wrong? / Welcher Satz ist falsch? 139

a) Charles invited many people to his wedding. ☐
b) Charles asked many people to his wedding. ☐
c) Charles had many people at his wedding. ☐
d) Charles visited many people to his wedding. ☐

Fill in ordinal numbers. / Fügen Sie Ordinalzahlen ein. 140

a) This is their ___________ Christmas as a family, as their first child was born last month.
b) Stephanie was ___________ in the competition and received the bronze medal.

c) One more than four times is the ___________ time.

d) The last day of May is the ___________ .

e) The year 1996 is at the end of the ___________ century.

141 **Fill in the prepositions. / Setzen Sie die Präpositionen ein.**

a) The party lasted ___________ midnight.

b) The day ___________ Tuesday is Monday.

c) They are getting married ___________ Saturday.

d) She can stay ___________ only ten minutes.

e) Harry gets up ___________ six o'clock every morning.

f) I shall arrive ___________ two hours.

g) My parents will visit us ___________ the weekend.

142 **When does it happen? / Wann geschieht es?**

a) When you are alive, your heart ___________ beats.

b) The sun sets ___________ evening.

c) It ___________ snows in Ethiopia.

d) A total eclipse of the sun takes place very ___________ .

e) In a metropolis the ___________ buzzing of traffic never stops.

f) The church bells toll ___________ every hour.

143 **Fill in the gaps. / Vervollständigen Sie die Sätze.**

celebrate *outing* *national anthem* *sports events* *national holiday*
open air *fireworks* *events* *performances*

The fourth of July is the _____________ of the United States of America. Many special _____________ take place on that day. If the weather is good, most Americans _____________ the day outside. Families will get together for an _____________ in the country or meet in a park to listen to one of the many _____________ concerts.

The opera houses in the big cities present gala _____________ by famous singers and there are special _____________ in the stadiums. When the _____________ is played at the beginning of the events the audience stands up respectfully.

For most Americans the highlights of the day, however, are the spectacular ______________ that light up the night sky all over the country.

Choose the right word. / Wählen Sie das richtige Wort. 144

a) Gary visited his father **while/during** the Christmas holidays.

b) We heard a **strange/foreign** noise in the basement.

c) Phil **ready/finished** cooking before his guest arrived.

d) I always **stand up/get up** late on Sunday mornings.

e) The **end/stop** of the film was tragic.

f) Venus is one of the brightest stars in the evening **heaven/sky**.

Give an antonym for each word. / Nennen Sie jeweils ein Antonym (einen Gegensatz). 145

a) merry ______________

b) lucky ______________

c) exciting ______________

d) peaceful ______________

e) lonely ______________

f) quiet ______________

Which sentence is wrong? / Welcher Satz ist falsch? 146

a) They are hoping for good weather. ☐

b) She made a wish upon a star. ☐

c) They want to go after Paris. ☐

d) I dream of a white Christmas. ☐

Which sentence is right? / Welcher Satz ist richtig? 147

a) We long after a quiet hotel. ☐

b) We long at a quiet hotel. ☐

c) We long in a quiet hotel. ☐

d) We long for a quiet hotel. ☐

The Weather / Das Wetter

148 **Translate the following. / Übersetzen Sie folgende Begriffe.**

a) null Grad ____________________
b) die Wettervorhersage ____________________
c) der Gefrierpunkt ____________________
d) Celsius ____________________
e) Temperatur ____________________
f) Luft ____________________
g) Klima ____________________

149 **Connect the matching expressions. / Verbinden Sie die passenden Begriffe.**

a) a dewy	hurricane
b) the scorching heat of the	frost
c) a raging	snow
d) the melting	sunshine
e) a keen	early morning
f) glorious	dog-days

150 **Fill in the missing words. / Ergänzen Sie die Sätze.**

hailstones lightning weather map rainbow icicles avalanche

a) The ______________ in the newspaper showed a low over England.
b) The ______________ hanging from the eaves looked like arrows of glass.
c) Last December an ______________ came down the mountain and destroyed the winter resort.
d) The tree went up in flames after it was struck by ______________ .
e) When the sun shone through the rain clouds there was a beautiful ______________ in the sky.
f) The roofs of many cars were damaged by ______________ as large as walnuts.

Which sentence is correct? / Welcher Satz ist richtig? 151

a) The football match was cancelled due to strong rainfall. ☐

b) The football match was cancelled due to heavy rainfall. ☐

c) The football match was cancelled due to many rainfall. ☐

d) The football match was cancelled due to serious rainfall. ☐

What is a single one of these phenomena called? / Wie heißt nur ein einziges dieser Phänomene? 152

a) a ________ of thunder

b) a ________ of sunshine

c) a ________ of lightning

d) a ________ of wind

Which word does not fit? / Welches Wort paßt nicht? 153

a) hail, sleet, dew, snowflakes, snow-pellets

b) fog, mist, overcast, haze

c) gloomy, dull, cloudy, violent, grey

d) fine, fair, blond, beautiful, sunny, golden

e) howl, stride, whistle, rage, blow

What is it? / Was ist das? 154

a) It can ruin pot plants in late autumn. ____________

b) A very heavy snowstorm is a ____________.

c) The earth moves and cracks in an ____________.

d) It covers everything in water after extended rainfalls. ____________

e) A very long period without rain is a ____________.

Name four compound words that begin with *snow*. / Nennen Sie vier zusammengesetzte Wörter, die mit *snow* anfangen. 155

__________________ __________________

__________________ __________________

156 **Which sentence has a different meaning? / Welcher Satz bedeutet etwas anderes?**

a) I am cold. ☐

b) I am chilly. ☐

c) I have a cold. ☐

d) I feel cold. ☐

157 **Which word does not rhyme? / Welches Wort reimt nicht?**

a) clear, pier, here, cheer, there, near, deer

b) high, rye, day, tie, cry, my, buy

c) pour, tore, door, pore, adore, yore, your

d) shine, fine, sign, deign, encline, opine

e) rain, insane, pane, feign, Spain, can

f) sleet, counterfeit, appetite, eat, bleat, feet

g) toe, mow, tomato, sew, grow, stew, plateau, foe

158 **What do the following idioms mean? Was bedeuten diese Sprichwörter?**

a) It never rains but it pours. ______________________________

b) It's raining cats and dogs. ______________________________

c) to save up for a rainy day ______________________________

d) a storm in a teacup ______________________________

e) to get wind of something ______________________________

f) to see how the wind blows ______________________________

g) under the weather ______________________________

159 **Name five compound words that begin with *rain*. / Nennen Sie fünf zusammengesetzte Wörter, die mit *rain* anfangen.**

____

____

____

____

____

The adjectives in these sentences have become mixed up. Put them in the right place. / Die Adjektive in diesen Sätzen sind verrutscht. Setzen Sie sie richtig ein. 160

a) The ground was still **overcast** after the rain. ___________

b) The **foggy** wind blew off his hat. ___________

c) The waves were very low in the **wet** ocean. ___________

d) Vision was seriously limited on that **billowing** day. ___________

e) April was marked by highly **calm** weather - there was everything from glorious sunshine to severe snowstorms. ___________

f) Not one ray of sun penetrated the **changeable** sky. ___________

The Human Body / Der Mensch

Name the part of the body. / Nennen Sie den Körperteil. 161

a) You see with your ________________.

b) You smell with your ________________.

c) You chew with your ________________.

d) You think with your ________________.

e) You hold something in your ________________.

f) You sit on your ________________.

g) You carry a rucksack on your ________________.

These are questions a doctor might ask you. Put the words in the right order. / Diese Fragen könnte Ihnen eine Ärztin stellen. Bringen Sie sie in die richtige Reihenfolge. 162

a) for can I you do what ? ______________________________

b) you open would your please mouth ? ______________________________

c) I press does hurt it here if ? ______________________________

d) had you with it trouble before have ? ______________________________

e) pregnant could be you ? ______________________________

f) does often how pain come back the ? ______________________________

g) mouth would rinse your you please ? ______________________________

163 **Of which parts of the body do you have ten each? / Von welchen Körperteilen haben sie jeweils zehn?**

__________________ __________________

____

164 **What are *limbs*? / Was sind *limbs* ?**

a) the little bumps that appear on one's skin when one is cold ☐

b) the pants of a servant's uniform ☐

c) the arms and legs of a human being ☐

d) the small folds in the skin that come with age ☐

165 **Match the German and the English. / Verbinden Sie die englischen Begriffe mit der deutschen Übersetzung.**

a) respiration	Schläfe
b) appendix	Wade
c) calf	Niere
d) bile	Atmung
e) temple	Blinddarm
f) kidney	Galle

166 **Fill in the right word. / Setzen Sie das passende Wort ein.**

carry wear waste waists pail pale way weigh

a) He is very _________ because he has just had the flu.

b) She filled a _________ of water and washed her car.

c) Could you please show me the _________ to the hospital?

d) I think I _________ about five pounds more now.

e) Women have smaller _________ than men.

f) Don't _________ your money on ineffective diets.

g) Do you _________ contact lenses?

h) Due to a bad back I cannot _________ heavy objects.

167 **What is it called? / Wie heißt es?**

a) to breathe heavily is to __________________

b) to look intensely is to ______________

c) to listen secretly is to ______________

d) to look cross-eyed is to ______________

e) to speak with involuntary repetitions is to ______________

f) to hold on tightly is to ______________

g) to walk with difficulty is to ______________

Which word does not fit? / Welches Wort paßt nicht? 168

a) pain, hurt, suffering, pale, ache, agony, pang

b) mind, soul, spirit, brain, ghost

c) to slumber, to lose one's senses, to sleep, to take a nap

d) robust, reserved, healthy, vigorous, sound

Which sentence has a different meaning? / Welcher Satz bedeutet etwas anderes? 169

a) He had a very arrogant countenance. ☐

b) He had a very arrogant expression. ☐

c) He had very arrogant behaviour. ☐

d) He had very arrogant features. ☐

What are these disorders called? / Wie heißen diese Störungen? 170

a) If you cannot speak you are ____________ .

b) If you cannot see you are ____________ .

c) If you cannot hear you are ____________ .

d) If you cannot feel you are ____________ .

e) If you cannot move you are ____________ .

Fill in the gaps. / Setzen Sie das passende Wort ein. 171

iris *pupil* *eyelids* *eyelashes* *eyebrows* *blind spot*

a) The line of hair above the eyes are the ____________ .

b) You close your ____________ when you go to sleep.

c) Long ____________ are said to be very attractive.

d) One's ____________ can be brown, blue or green.

e) If you look into somebody's ___________ , you can usually see a tiny image of yourself in it.

f) The little area on the retina with which one cannot see is the ________ .

172 **Fill in the prepositions. / Fügen Sie die Präpositionen ein.**

a) Don't eat or drink anything ___________ four hours.

b) Could I have something ___________ the pain, please?

c) The pain should have disappeared ___________ twelve hours.

d) I cannot give you an appointment ___________ December.

e) Eating a balanced diet will build ___________ your immune system.

f) We must keep you ___________ observation for a few days.

g) Try to read the symbols ___________ that chart.

173 **Connect the halves. / Verbinden Sie die Satzhälften.**

to catch	some ointment
to visit	a cold
to be afflicted by	a doctor
to deliver	a tumour
to take a turn for	an autopsy
to perform	a child
to remove	the worse
to apply	a hereditary disease

174 **Arrange these body parts in the same order in which they appear on a human. / Ordnen Sie diese Körperteile in der Reihenfolge, die sie am Körper einnehmen.**

a) knuckles, wrist, nails, palm ______________________________

b) ankle, toe, calf, thigh, knee ______________________________

c) palate, lips, e(o)sophagus, stomach ________________________

175 **Fill in the right word. / Setzen Sie das richtige Wort ein.**

box *case* *spell* *bark* *blow*

a) That ________ on the head made him feel dizzy.

b) Some natural medicines are made from the ________ of trees.

c) One should keep one's first aid kit in a sturdy ________ .

d) The witch doctor cast an ancient ________ on his patient.

e) That is the worst ________ of the measles I have seen this year.

f) That boy always ________ es his little brother when their parents aren't watching.

g) If Mommy ________ s on that hurt, it will feel better.

h) You may take two ________ s and a handbag on the plane.

i) Could you ________ that French word, please?

j) Their dog always ________ s when cars pass.

Where are these parts of the body? / Wo befinden sich diese Körperteile? 176

a) the gums are in the ____________________

b) the womb is in the ____________________

c) a molar is in the ____________________

d) the skull is in the ____________________

e) a vertebra is a part of the ____________________

f) the intestines are in the ____________________

g) the cheeks are in the ____________________

h) the nostrils are in the ____________________

Which sentence has a different meaning? / Welcher Satz hat eine andere Bedeutung? 177

a) I feel sick. ☐

b) My stomach is upset. ☐

c) I feel nauseous. ☐

d) I am sick. ☐

Connect the word with its definition. / Verbinden Sie das Wort mit seiner Bedeutung. 178

a) vaccination/inoculation	a minor injury that causes the skin to change colour temporarily

b) indigestion	an irritation or inflammation of the skin
c) rash	a method by which the body is made immune to certain diseases
d) flatulence	a condition during which the stomach cannot tolerate certain foods
e) a cast	a condition during which gases are produced in the stomach or the intestines
f) a bruise	a dressing made with plaster of paris that is applied to broken bones

179 **Name one word for the following parts of the body. / Nennen Sie den Überbegriff für diese Körperteile.**

a) incisors, canines, bicuspids, molars ________________

b) knuckles, elbows, shoulders, knees ________________

c) heart, liver, lungs, stomach, gall-bladder ________________

180 **Choose the right word. / Wählen Sie das richtige Wort.**

a) You must take those pills every day of the week/weak.

b) Do not get up if you are feeling week/weak.

c) That cut will heel/heal faster if you do not cover it.

d) My new shoes gave me a blister on my left heel/heal.

e) He felt a sharp pane/pain in his ankle after the jump.

f) The window panes/pains were shattered by the explosion.

181 **What are the opposites of the marked words? / Was ist das Gegenteil der hervorgehobenen Wörter?**

a) to be **cold** ________________

b) to **shiver from cold** ________________

c) a **benign** tumour ________________

d) a **contagious** disease ________________

e) to be of **poor** health ________________

f) to be **emaciated** ____________

g) to **build up** the immune system ____________

Fill in the English word. / Setzen Sie das englische Wort ein. 182

a) The wound was so big that he needed __________ (genäht werden).

b) It is an art to apply a __________ (Verband) to the hand correctly.

c) If you have a cast on your foot you need __________ (Krücken) to walk.

d) The little boy wanted a __________ (Pflaster) on every little scratch.

e) The pirates in fairy tales often wear __________ (Augenklappen).

Name four parts of the foot. / Nennen Sie vier Teile des Fußes. 183

____________ ____________

____________ ____________

Translate these words. / Übersetzen Sie folgende Worte. 184

a) ____________ eine Narbe

b) ____________ Sonnenstich

c) baldness ____________

d) an ointment ____________

e) ____________ in Ohnmacht fallen

f) dizziness ____________

g) dentures ____________

h) ____________ sich räuspern

Fill in the gaps. / Ergänzen Sie die Sätze. 185

lethal hereditary allergy infectious epidemic

a) The plague was an __________ .

b) Hayfever is an __________ .

c) Cancer is often __________ .

d) The colour of one's eyes is __________ .

e) A real influenza is very __________ .

186 **Connect the halves. / Verbinden Sie die Hälften.**

a) A paediatrician	is a doctor who operates
b) A dermatologist	is a doctor for the mind
c) A gynaecologist	is a doctor for the teeth
d) An orthopaedist	is a doctor for general diseases
e) A dentist	is a doctor for the skin
f) A psychiatrist	is a doctor for the bones
g) A general practitioner	is a doctor for children
h) A surgeon	is a doctor for women

187 **Which names of medical instruments are hidden in these mixed-up words? / Die Namen welcher medizinischer Instrumente sind in diesen Buchstaben versteckt?**

a) scopeethost ____________________	amplifies the sounds of the body
b) llidr ____________________	carves holes in teeth for fillings
c) doolb-ssurepre tusraappa ________	measures the blood-pressure
d) ary-X rapatusap ________________	takes pictures of bones
e) ygoxen kmas ____________________	helps one breathe in an emergency
f) risynge ____________________	is used to inject medication
g) bacutorin ____________________	houses premature babies

188 **Connect the English idioms with the German. / Verbinden Sie die englischen Redewendungen mit der deutschen Erklärung.**

a) to swallow the pill	mit Hängen und Würgen
b) to speak one's mind	mündlich
c) by the skin of ones teeth	davon läuft es mir kalt den Rücken runter
d) that gives me the shivers	dem Tode nahe
e) an eye for an eye, a tooth for a tooth	nervös sein
f) at death's door	der Zankapfel
g) to be the apple of one's eye	die Meinung sagen
h) the bone of contention	jemandem besonders lieb sein

i) to have butterflies in one's stomach
j) by word of mouth

Auge um Auge, Zahn um Zahn
in den sauren Apfel beißen

Sports and Games / Sport und Spiel

Fill in the gaps. / Ergänzen Sie diese Sätze. 189

a) What kind of sport do you ____________ (treiben)?
b) When does the ____________ (Wettspiel) start?
c) What is the ____________ (Spielstand)?
d) It's a ____________ (Heimspiel).
e) She played on our ____________ (Seite).
f) The two top ____________ (Mannschaften) can still win the competition.
g) Are you a ____________ (Mitglied) of a sports club?
h) I engage in sports for ____________ (Erholung) only.

Which sport is it? / Welche Sportart ist es? 190

a) one jumps from a tower into water ____________
b) two groups of eleven people chase a ball across a field ____________
c) one runs on ice with special shoes ____________
d) two people play with kings, queens and pawns ____________
e) one slides down snow-covered mountain slopes ____________
f) two people do it to music on a wooden floor ____________
g) one jumps over obstacles on a track ____________
h) two people attack each other with fists ____________
i) one jumps from a plane with an umbrella-shaped device ____________

Where does one play these sports? / Wo werden diese Sportarten gespielt? 191

a) football on a ________________________
b) athletics on an ________________________
c) golf on a ________________________

d) tennis on a ______________________

e) car-racing on a ______________________

f) swimming in a ______________________

g) shooting in a ______________________

h) boxing in a ______________________

i) figure skating in a ______________________

j) surfing in the ______________________

192 **Which device do you need to play these sports? / Was benötigen Sie, um diese Sportarten zu treiben?**

a) fishing a ______________

b) golf a ______________

c) boxing ______________

d) fencing a/n ______________

e) hockey a ______________

f) sledging a ______________

g) skiing a pair of ______________

h) pole vaulting a ______________

i) cricket a ______________

j) tennis a ______________

k) riding a ______________

l) archery a ______________

m) weight-lifting ______________

193 **What are the competitions in these sports called? / Wie heißt ein Wettbewerb in diesen Sportarten?**

a) hockey ______________

b) yachting ______________

c) figure skating ______________

d) tennis ______________

e) football ______________

f) competitions of the best athletes in the world ______________

Give one synonym for each word. / Nennen Sie jeweils ein Synonym. 194

a) graceful ________________

b) muscular ________________

c) fast ________________

d) accurate ________________

e) to agree ________________

f) to enjoy ________________

g) to beat ________________

Name four positions in a soccer team. / Nennen Sie vier Positionen in einer Fußballmannschaft. 195

________________ ________________

________________ ________________

What is not a definition of *match*? / Was ist keine Definition von *match*? 196

a) a person or thing similar to another ☐

b) a contest between two or more people or groups ☐

c) a marriage union ☐

d) an instrument for recording humidity ☐

e) a small piece of wood tipped with combustible material ☐

Give an antonym for each word. / Nennen Sie ein Antonym für jedes Wort. 197

a) thoughtful ________________

b) selfish ________________

c) successful ________________

d) obedient ________________

e) fearful ________________

f) polite ________________

g) perfect ________________

h) kind ________________

i) faithful ________________

198 **Fill in the gaps. / Ergänzen Sie die Lücken.**

score kick-off referee title cup goal

a) The football game started with the ________ at 2 p.m.

b) The ________ decided that the goal was not valid.

c) A Russian teenager held the ________ „World Champion“ for two years.

d) At the prize-giving the champion kissed the ________ she had just won.

e) The ________ of the volleyball match was 4-0.

f) Our ice-hockey team lost because the puck did not enter the ________ once.

199 **Translate the names of these games. / Übersetzen Sie die Namen dieser Spiele.**

a) ping-pong ________________

b) draughts (UK), checkers (US) ________________

c) badminton ________________

d) bowling ________________

e) darts ________________

f) hide-and-seek ________________

g) seesawing ________________

200 **Fill in the English word. / Fügen Sie das englische Wort ein.**

a) This game is for ________ (Spieler/innen) aged nine to ninety-nine.

b) The players take turns at throwing the ________ (Würfel).

c) One must ________ (mischen) the cards thoroughly after each game.

d) Chess, draughts and Monopoly are ________ (Brettspiele).

e) Children love to fly ________ (Drachen) on windy autumn days.

f) The ________ (Lösung) to the crossword puzzle was rather difficult.

g) The ________ (Zauberer) pulled six living chickens out of the hat.

h) The perfect little ________ (Puppenhaus) is even equipped with electricity.

201 **Name the colour of these symbols in a card game. / Welche Farbe haben diese Karten?**

a) hearts ________

b) diamonds ________
c) spades ________
d) clubs ________

Where do you find these things? / Wo würden Sie folgende Dinge antreffen? 202

swings, a seesaw, a sandbox, a roundabout at a ____________

Fill in the right idiomatic expression with *keep* or *kick*. / Fügen Sie den richtigen idiomatischen Begriff mit *keep* oder *kick* ein. 203

kicked him out *kicked up a fuss* *kept his word* *kept on*
keep me company *keep away from* *kept a straight face*
keep your head

a) Please, stay and ____________ (be with me) for a while.
b) Nobody ____________ (stayed serious) in that funny situation.
c) The coach ____________ (didn't stop talking) about the mistakes the team had made.
d) Always ____________ (remain calm), even if you are many points behind.
e) Father ____________ (carried out his promise) and took the children swimming on Sunday.
f) ____________ (don't go near) the net if you want to return any balls.
g) They ____________ (expelled) of the team because he always lost his temper.
h) The fans ________ (became loud) after the umpire had made his decision.

Animals / Tiere

Which animal is it? / Welches Tier ist es? 204

a) It has yellow and black stripes.
It is an insect.
It makes honey. ______________
b) It is black and white.

It is a bird.
One says that it brings babies. ______________

c) It has a trunk.
It is very small.
It can keep you awake all night. ______________

d) It is long and thin.
It has no legs.
You can die if it bites you. ______________

e) It lives in the sea.
It is a mammal.
It has helped people in need. ______________

f) It has grey fur.
It can fly.
Dracula turns into one sometimes. ______________

g) It lives in icy water.
It has very warm fur.
It barks almost like a dog. ______________

h) It eats leaves.
It lives in Africa.
It has a very long neck. ______________

i) It is big and grey.
It has bad eyesight.
It has a horn on its nose. ______________

205 **Fill in the missing name of the male or female animal. / Ergänzen Sie die männliche oder die weibliche Form.**

male	female
a) ________	hen
b) ________	duck
c) gander	________
d) dog	________
e) ________	sow
f) ________	she-goat

g) fox ________

h) lion ________

Fill in the prepositions. / Ergänzen Sie die Präpositionen. 206

Yesterday Dad took the children ________ the zoo. Mom could not join them because she had too much work to do ________ her office.

There were many animals ________ the zoo. Some were kept ________ cages, others ________ more spacious outside enclosures.

The children saw a lazy brown bear that lay ________ her back in the sun all day, while her little cubs climbed ________ her face and her tummy all the time. All they saw of the polar bear were two twinkling eyes, because he hid from the sun ________ a cave.

There was much noise in the penguin pen, as those little busy-bodies constantly jumped ________ their swimming-pool and then climbed ________ it again.

The children loved the monkeys and Dad had much trouble getting them ________ the monkey cage. In the evening it was even more difficult to get the children ________ the zoo and to go home.

Arrange from the smallest to the biggest. / Ordnen Sie die Tiere vom kleinsten zum größten. 207

squirrel, mite, eagle, rhinoceros, blue whale, flea, wild boar

____

Fill in the gaps. / Ergänzen Sie die Lücken. 208

mammals *rodents* *migratory birds* *amphibians* *mongrel* *beasts of prey*

a) Animals that kill others for food are ________________ .

b) ________________ fly to warm countries in winter.

c) ________________ can live on land as well as in water.

d) The animals that give birth to living young are ________________ .

e) The order of small gnawing animals are the ________________ .

f) A cross between two breeds of animals is a ________________ .

209 **What is the young of these animals called? / Wie heißt das Junge dieser Tiere?**

a) dog ____________
b) cat ____________
c) chicken ____________
d) sheep ____________
e) pig ____________
f) goat ____________
g) cow ____________
h) lion ____________
i) bear ____________
j) horse ____________

210 **Translate the following. / Übersetzen Sie folgendes.**

a) Please, do not feed the animals. ____________
b) Beware of the dog! ____________
c) Do not enter the cage! ____________
d) No entry. ____________

211 **Connect the halves. / Verbinden Sie die Satzhälften.**

a) A dove	squeaks.
b) A sheep	howls.
c) A wolf	crows.
d) A crow	hisses.
e) A cock	bleats.
f) A mouse	caws.
g) A snake	hums.
h) A bee	coos.

212 **Put the subjects of these sentences in the right place. / Setzen Sie das verrutschte Subjekt dieser Sätze zurück in den richtigen Satz.**

a) **A hippopotamus** was perched on the cherry tree.

____

b) **The swallow** carried the explorer's luggage across the desert.

____

c) **A camel** flew circles around the rosebush.

____

d) **The butterfly** gives wool for warm pullovers.

____

e) **A sheep** went for a walk underwater.

____

Which sentence is wrong? / Welcher Satz ist falsch? 213

a) The lions devoured the zebra in only thirty minutes. ☐
b) The lions ate the zebra in only thirty minutes. ☐
c) The lions dined on the zebra in only thirty minutes. ☐
d) The lions fed on the zebra for only thirty minutes. ☐
e) The lions consumed the zebra in only thirty minutes. ☐

What noises do these animals make? / Welche Geräusche machen diese Tiere? 214

a) dogs ________________
b) cats ________________
c) cows ________________
d) lions ________________
e) birds ________________
f) frogs ________________
g) nightingales ________________
h) ducks ________________

Choose the right word. / Wählen Sie das richtige Wort. 215

a) A **donkey/easel** carried our luggage up the mountain.
b) The farmer fertilised the fields with **mist/manure** from his own stables.
c) The children took their new **doll/puppy** for a walk on a leash.
d) He made much money **handling/trading** in tarantulas.

e) A **snake/snail** carries its house on its back.

f) The seal was trained to **wave/wink** good-bye with its flippers.

216 **Connect the animals with their houses. / Verbinden Sie das Tier mit seinem Haus.**

a) Bears live in a	cobweb.
b) Blackbirds live in a	lodge.
c) Beavers live in a	shell.
d) Bees live in a	warren.
e) Rabbits live in a	den.
f) Spiders live in a	hive.
g) Snails live in a	nest.

217 **Fill in the gaps. / Ergänzen Sie die Lücken.**

muzzle locusts pigeons pedigree pets rats

a) Cats and dogs are the most popular ______________ in Europe.

b) ______________ were used to carry letters in the Middle Ages.

c) The Pied Piper lured all the ______________ out of the city of Hameln.

d) If your dog bites it must wear a ______________ .

e) All thoroughbred animals have a long ______________ .

f) The crop was destroyed by a swarm of ______________ .

218 **All these idioms use the word *bird* or *dog*. Fill in the right word. / Diese Sprichwörter und Redewendungen werden alle mit *bird* oder *dog* gebildet. Fügen Sie das richtige Wort ein.**

a) ________ of a feather flock together.
Dt.: Gleich und Gleich gesellt sich gern.

b) To kill two ________ with one stone.
Dt.: Zwei Fliegen mit einer Klappe schlagen.

c) It's raining cats and ________ .
Dt.: Es regnet Bindfäden.

d) To go to the ________ .
Dt.: Auf den Hund kommen.

e) Every ________ has its day.

Dt.: Jede/r hat mal eine Glückssträhne.

f) The early ________ catches the worm.

Dt.: Morgenstund hat Gold im Mund.

g) You can't teach an old ________ new tricks.

Dt.: Was Hänschen nicht lernt, lernt Hans nimmermehr.

Which word does not fit? / Welches Wort paßt nicht? 219

a) duck, goose, turtle, turkey, chicken

b) Alsatian, dachshund, poodle, greyhound, squirrel, cocker spaniel

c) magpie, vulture, lark, titmouse, shark, gull

d) giraffe, tiger, lioness, kitten, Siamese cat

e) salmon, pike, trout, beetle, carp, herring

f) moth, worm, grasshopper, locust, horsefly, spider

Which sentence is wrong? / Welcher Satz ist falsch? 220

a) Karen opened the cages and set all the animals free. ☐

b) Karen opened the cages and freed all the animals. ☐

c) Karen opened the cages and released all the animals. ☐

d) Karen opened the cages and fled all the animals. ☐

Derive nouns from the following words. / Bilden Sie aus den Wörtern Substantive (Hauptwörter). 221

a) A person who **works** is a ________________ .

b) A person who **acts** is an ________________ .

c) A person who **drives** is a ________________ .

d) A person who **assists** is an ________________ .

e) A person who **inhabits** is an ________________ .

f) A person who **explores** is an ________________ .

g) A person who is **employed** is an ________________ .

h) A person who **examines** is an ________________ .

i) A person who is being **examined** is an ________________ .

j) The act of **examining** is the ________________ .

k) The institution that **organises** is the ______________ .

l) The act of **imitating** is the ______________ .

222 **Choose the right word. / Wählen Sie das richtige Wort.**

a) Leopards and cheetahs **look/see** very much alike.

b) In Africa one can **listen/hear** the hyenas cackle at night.

c) Each tiger eats twenty pounds of **flesh/meat** every day.

d) Our beautiful St. Bernhard won a **price/prize** at the show.

e) Do you know **what/how** many stripes a zebra has?

f) The farmer's entire **cabbage/coal** harvest was eaten by rabbits.

223 **What is not a definition of *pen*? / Was ist keine Definition von *pen*?**

a) a small enclosure for animals ☐

b) an instrument for writing ☐

c) a female swan ☐

d) a needle used to fasten separate articles together ☐

e) the colloquial word for prison ☐

224 **Connect the word with its definition. / Verbinden Sie das Wort mit seiner Bedeutung.**

a) trunk	an animal that is caught by another for food
b) prey	the many small flat plates that cover a fish's body
c) fangs	the hard, rigid cover of an a tortoise's body
d) scales	the mouth of a bird
e) bill	the long, tubelike muscle that elephants use for sucking
f) shell	the long, sharp teeth that animals use to tear prey

225 **What do these idioms mean? / Was bedeuten diese Sprichwörter?**

a) He is as dead as a dodo.

____

b) To shut the door when the horse has bolted.

____

c) To have kittens.

____

d) To have a whale of a time.

____

e) To behave like a bull in a china shop.

____

f) To be as mad as a March hare.

____

What is a *caterpillar*? / Was ist ein *caterpillar*? 226

a) a young animal fattened for slaughter

b) the larva of a butterfly or a moth

c) a supporting column in a building

d) the name of a tractor that moves on two steel belts and not on wheels

What do you call a group of these animals? / Wie heißt eine Gruppe dieser Tiere? 227

pack flight family herd school swarm

a) a ______________ of elephants

b) a ______________ of bees

c) a ______________ of wolves

d) a ______________ of dolphins

e) a ______________ of birds

f) a ______________ of lions

Plants / Pflanzen

Fill in the prepositions. / Setzen Sie die Präpositionen ein. 228

a) I must put the bouquet ________ a vase.

b) Red currants grow ________ bushes.

c) Our yard is covered ________ weeds.

d) He was impressed ________ the beauty of her rose garden.

e) Pineapples are indigenous ________ tropical regions.

f) They dream ________ a house with a pretty garden.

229 **Match the English word with the German. / Verbinden Sie das englische Wort mit seiner deutschen Bedeutung.**

a) daisy	Maiglöckchen
b) cornflower	Narzisse
c) daffodil	Nelke
d) dandelion	Kornblume
e) lily of the valley	Vergißmeinnicht
f) carnation	Gänseblümchen
g) forget-me-not	Löwenzahn

230 **Fill in the gaps. / Ergänzen Sie die Lücken.**

grains seeds buds blooms blossoms

a) In spring the cherry ______________ in Washington attract many tourists.

b) Crocus ______________ are the first flowers that appear in spring.

c) The ______________ of a dandelion can fly very far.

d) The field mouse collected ______________ of wheat for the winter.

e) All the daffodils burst from their ______________ on the first warm day of spring.

231 **Match the English and the German expressions. / Verbinden Sie den englischen Begriff mit seiner deutschen Bedeutung.**

a) core and kernel	Stamm und Ast
b) husk and chaff	Gehäuse und Kern
c) trunk and branch	Stiel und Schale
d) stalk and peel	Stumpf und gefällter Baumstamm
e) stump and log	Hülse und Spreu

Fill in the right word. / Fügen Sie das richtige Wort ein. 232

skin petal peel shell

a) the ________ of a nut

b) the ________ of a potato

c) the ________ of a peach

d) the ________ of a rose

Which sentence has a different meaning? / Welcher Satz hat eine andere Bedeutung? 233

a) The fragrance of these flowers reminds me of my grandmother's garden. ☐

b) The shape of these flowers reminds me of my grandmother's garden. ☐

c) The scent of these flowers reminds me of my grandmother's garden. ☐

d) The smell of these flowers reminds me of my grandmother's garden. ☐

e) The perfume of these flowers reminds me of my grandmother's garden. ☐

Match the word and its definition. / Verbinden Sie das Wort mit seiner Definition. 234

a) vegetable plant	trees that lose their leaves in winter
b) ornamental shrub	the swollen, round part of plants (such as tulips) that is underground
c) coniferous tree	a small, fleshy plant with a stem and a cap
d) bulbs	a plant grown for a part that will be eaten
e) edible mushrooms	evergreen trees that have cones
f) deciduous trees	a bush grown for its beauty

What is a *weed*? / Was ist ein *weed*? 235

a) the swollen, round part of plants that is underground ☐

b) the skin between a duck's toes ☐

c) a fast-growing plant of no value ☐

d) a cannibalistic louse found in Northern Europe ☐

236 **Fill in the gaps. / Ergänzen Sie die Lücken.**

admire *fade* *bunch* *scent*

People love to be surprised with a _______ of flowers. The _______ of some flowers can fill an entire room with a pleasant smell. Unfortunately, there is only little time to _______ the beauty of cut flowers, because they lose their freshness and _______ after a few days.

237 **Find the names of ten flowers hidden here. / Welche zehn Blumen haben sich hier versteckt?**

s	t	v	i	o	l	e	t	a	r	g
p	e	o	n	y	o	k	u	b	s	e
o	r	g	e	d	u	n	l	a	b	n
d	g	i	r	i	s	u	i	e	e	t
a	u	r	m	e	l	l	p	s	a	i
i	n	u	d	r	e	s	t	a	n	a
s	u	n	f	l	o	w	e	r	y	n
y	n	o	t	h	e	s	r	e	g	u
p	l	b	l	u	e	b	e	l	l	e
a	s	e	p	h	o	n	e	m	e	n
w	o	e	d	e	l	w	e	i	s	s

238 **Which word does not fit? / Welches Wort paßt nicht?**

a) lily, poppy, pansy, cabbage, bluebell

b) pumpkin, asparagus, bean, leek, buttercup

c) bamboo, date, plum, banana, pear, quince

d) oak, beach, rice, maple, poplar

239 **Fill in the gaps. / Ergänzen Sie die Lücken.**

mistletoe *bark* *toadstools* *foliage* *needles* *ebony* *vine*

a) People who meet under a _______________ at Christmas must kiss.

b) The darkest coloured wood is ______________ .

c) Birch trees have a white ______________ .

d) Fir and pine trees don't have leaves, but ______________ .

e) In winter all deciduous trees loose their ______________ .

f) Grapes grow on a ______________ .

g) ______________ are poisonous mushrooms.

Connect the two halves of the words. / Verbinden Sie die Worthälften. 240

a) rose – berry
b) pine bean
c) blue – root
d) sun cone
e) beet – bud
f) mush – flower
g) coffee – room

Fill in the right verb. / Fügen Sie das richtige Verb ein. 241

produce increase perform protect maintain

a) The aim of Greenpeace is to ______________ nature.

b) It is allowed to ______________ genetic manipulation on plants in most countries.

c) Every government should try to ______________ the ecological balance in its country.

d) The exhaust fumes of cars ______________ acid rain.

e) Propellant gases used in spray cans ______________ the size of the ozone hole.

Give one antonym for each word. / Nennen Sie ein Antonym für jedes Wort. 242

a) beautiful ______________

b) fragrance ______________

c) fertile ______________

d) colourful ______________

e) underground ____________

f) rough ____________

Travelling and Transportation / Reise und Verkehr

243 **Translate the following. / Übersetzen Sie folgendes.**

a) Bahnhof ____________

b) Flughafen ____________

c) Hafen ____________

d) Busbahnhof ____________

e) Parkplatz ____________

f) Fahrradstellplatz ____________

244 **What are the alternatives? / Was sind die Alternativen?**

a) a ____________ or a return ticket

b) a ____________ or an aisle seat

c) the smoking or the ____________ section

d) first or ____________ class

245 **Complete the sentences. / Ergänzen Sie die Sätze.**

a) How ____________ (kosten) a ticket to Detroit?

b) When does the first train ____________ (abfahren) in the morning?

c) Where can I ____________ (umtauschen) this ticket?

d) When do we ____________ (ankommen) in Bath?

e) Who will ____________ (kontrollieren) our passports?

f) Are you ____________ (reisen) alone?

246 **The words in these sentences are mixed up. Put them in the right order. / In diesen Sätzen sind die Wörter durcheinander. Ordnen Sie sie.**

a) free is seat this ? ____________

b) open I window may the? ____________

c) these please, in fill forms. ______________________________

d) six children are free under charge of. ______________________________

e) see I your may please ticket ? ______________________________

f) pleasant a have journey ! ______________________________

Connect the word with its definition. / Verbinden Sie das Wort mit seiner Definition. 247

a) couchette	the area from which you enter a train
b) supplement	the place at the end of a journey
c) platform	a passage between sections of seats
d) reduced rate	a train compartment with six narrow beds
e) souvenir	an additional price for special trains, ships etc.
f) destination	a cheaper price for children, students, etc.
g) aisle	something bought to remind one of a journey

Fill in the gaps. / Ergänzen Sie die Lücken. 248

arrival emergency duty-free left-luggage waiting room departure customs

a) Before a plane leaves the passengers wait in the ____________ .

b) The place where one leaves is the place of ____________ .

c) The place where a plane lands is the place of ____________ .

d) You pay taxes on imported goods at the ____________ office.

e) Things that can be imported without paying import taxes are _________ .

f) Lost suitcases are kept in the ____________ office.

g) In dangerous situations passengers can leave a plane through the ____________ exits.

Where do these people work? / Wo arbeiten diese Leute? 249

a) a travel agent	in a	____________________
b) a pilot	on a/an	____________________
c) a conductor	on a	____________________
d) an engine-driver	on a	____________________
e) a captain	on a	____________________

f) a skipper on a ________________

g) a sailor on a ________________

250 **Fill in the gaps.**

a) I can ride on all buses in this town for one month with a ________ ticket.

b) One sleeps in the sleeping ______________ of a night train.

c) A ship that carries cars across a river is a ______________ .

d) Trains that carry only goods are called ______________ trains.

e) All the stops of a train are listed in the ______________ .

251 **What is an *airliner*? / Was ist ein *airliner*?**

a) ein Verkehrsflugzeug ☐

b) ein Kondenzstreifen ☐

c) eine Tragfläche ☐

d) ein Flugschreiber ☐

e) ein Bordfunker ☐

252 **Fill in the gaps. / Ergänzen Sie die Lücken.**

goes *get off* *boarding* *bus stop* *take*

a) ________ bus number ten from the station.

b) Don't forget to buy your ticket when ________ the bus.

c) The bus ________ to the ice stadium.

d) The nearest ________ to my house is Berlin Street.

e) After you ________ the bus take the second street on the left.

253 **Do you recognise these things from a hotel? / Erkennen Sie diese Dinge aus einem Hotel?**

a) ledbou moro ________________ one rents it

b) moor yke ________________ one needs it for a room

c) talonctinen keabrstaf ________________ one has it in the morning

d) kewa-pu llca ________________ a service in the morning

e) orom rsecevi ________________ it is available all the time

f) retrpo ____________________ will help you carry

g) singwimm loop ____________________ for your recreation

Complete these idioms with phrases with *get*. / Ergänzen Sie die Sprichwörter mit Satzteilen mit *get*. 254

get along well *get out of bed* *get through* *got on his nerves*
get a word in *get over with* *get round*

a) The noise from the elevator ____________ (irritated him).

b) If we don't ____________ (find time) to it today it will be too late.

c) We ____________ (are friends) with all our neighbours.

d) The tour-guide talked so much, we could not ____________ (interrupt).

e) We didn't ____________ (start the day) before 10 a.m. once during our holidays.

f) I must ____________ (finish) this task quickly because my train leaves in twenty minutes.

g) It did not ____________ (make sense) to him that the entry was free.

Who is it? / Wer ist das? 255

a) ______________ takes goods across a border illegally

b) ______________ rides on a bus

c) ______________ rents a room in a hotel

d) ______________ shows holidaymakers the sights of a town

e) ______________ hides on a ship without paying the fare

f) ______________ travels to another place for pleasure

Fill in the prepositions. / Ergänzen Sie die Präpositionen. 256

a) They apologized _______ not waiting for us.

b) We will arrive _______ Charlotte at 8 p.m.

c) Tracy was disappointed _______ the view from her window.

d) Laura was impressed _______ the speed of the train.

e) This sunny weather is typical _______ Florence in the springtime.

f) You seem unhappy. What is wrong _______ you?

257 **What is a traffic jam? / Was ist ein *traffic jam*?**

a) a specialty from Bavaria made of cooked fruit ☐

b) the reduced price for small cars on a ferry ☐

c) the situation when too many cars block the street ☐

d) a very small dirt road ☐

258 **Fill in the missing word. / Fügen Sie das fehlende Wort ein.**

a) A train rides on two endless ___________ .

b) A strong ___________ pulls a train.

c) The separate sections of a passenger coach are the ___________ .

d) The person who checks the tickets on a train is the ___________ .

e) The beds in a night train are called ___________ .

259 **Connect the English and the German. / Verbinden Sie den englischen Begriff mit seiner deutschen Übersetzung.**

a) barge	Rettungsboot
b) sailing-ship	Schlepper
c) wreck	Fischdampfer mit Schleppnetz
d) life-boat	Wrack
e) raft	Lastkahn
f) steamer	Floß
g) trawler	Segelschiff
h) tug(boat)	Dampfer

260 **Fill in the gaps. / Ergänzen Sie die Lücken.**

gangway portholes quay oars buoys lighthouse

a) The ___________ was built on a rock in the sea.

b) Bright orange ___________ floating in the water guided the ships.

c) One needs ___________ to move a rowing boat.

d) The cargo is loaded into the ship from the ___________ .

e) Our cabin in the hull of the ship had two round ___________ as windows.

f) The passengers entered the ship via a ___________ .

Complete the English expression. / Ergänzen Sie die englischen Begriffe. 261

a) to ________ a ship	ein Schiff vom Stapel lassen
b) to ________ to sea	in See stechen
c) to ________ at a port	einen Hafen anlaufen
d) to ________ ashore	an Land gehen
e) to ________	(sich) einschiffen
f) to ________	kentern

What is it? / Was ist das? 262

a) the track where aeroplanes take off and land ________________
b) the engines of old planes that rotate very fast ________________
c) a large airbag that flies when filled with hot air ________________
d) a plane that has no engine ________________
e) the place where the pilot sits in a plane ________________
f) the machines that suck in air to make planes move ________________
g) a plane with a motor on its roof that can take off and land vertically ________________

What does *to cover distance* mean? / Was bedeutet *to cover distance*? 263

a) einen Weg zerstören ☐
b) eine Strecke hinter sich bringen ☐
c) mit einer großen Decke zudecken ☐
d) vor etwas fliehen ☐

Name the vehicle. / Nennen Sie das Fahrzeug. 264

a) a large motor vehicle that transports heavy loads ________________
b) a motorised two-wheeler ________________
c) a wagon for a passenger that is attached to b) ________________
d) a motorised four-wheeler for about four people ________________
e) a room with wheels that can be pulled by a car ________________

265 Name the parts of a car. / Nennen Sie die Teile eines Autos.

a) it makes a car stop ____________

b) it makes a loud noise to warn others ____________

c) it catches the mud that splashes up from the wheels ____________

d) one must use it while changing gears ____________

e) the sign with numbers on it that is attached to the front and the back of every car ____________

f) the light that flashes when you turn around a corner ____________

g) the rubber part of the wheel ____________

h) the container that holds the fuel ____________

266 What is the *dashboard* of a car? / Was ist das *dashboard* eines Autos?

a) a button which starts or adjusts a mechanism ☐

b) the panel that holds the steering wheel and the controls ☐

c) a box for spare parts ☐

d) a special frame that protects passengers against injury in an accident ☐

267 Complete the English expression. / Ergänzen Sie die englischen Begriffe.

a) to ____________ the gear	den Gang wechseln
b) the car ____________	das Auto hatte eine Panne
c) to ____________ a car	ein Auto heben
d) to ____________ a tire	einen Reifen wechseln
e) to check the ____________	die Zündung prüfen
f) to ____________ a ball-bearing	ein Kugellager schmieren

268 Which sentence has a different meaning? / Welcher Satz hat eine andere Bedeutung?

a) Don't underestimate the dangers of a German highway! ☐

b) Don't underestimate the hazards of a German highway! ☐

c) Don't underestimate the perils of a German highway! ☐

d) Don't underestimate the hostilities of a German highway! ☐

e) Don't underestimate the threats of a German highway! ☐

Match the English and the German. / Verbinden Sie das Deutsche mit dem Englischen. 269

a) accelerator
b) fuel consumption
c) headlight
d) bonnet
e) radiator
f) boot

Haube
Kühler
Kofferraum
Brennstoffverbrauch
Scheinwerfer
Gaspedal

Fill in either *break* or *drive*. / Fügen Sie entweder *break* oder *drive* ein. 270

a) to _______ the news to somebody
Dt.: eine Nachricht eröffnen
b) to _______ a wedge between them
Dt.: einen Keil zwischen sie treiben
c) to achieve a _______-through
Dt.: einen Durchbruch erzielen
d) to _______ someone crazy
Dt.: jemanden auf die Palme bringen
e) You know what I'm _______ at.
Dt.: Du weißt, worauf ich hinaus will.
f) to _______ away from something
Dt.: sich von etwas lösen
g) to _______ new ground
Dt.: Neuland betreten
h) to _______ something home to somebody
Dt.: jemandem etwas klar machen

Connect the questions with the right answers. / Verbinden Sie die Fragen mit den richtigen Antworten. 271

a) Q: I'd like a ticket to Freiburg, please.
A: No, it's free.
b) Q: Is this seat taken?
A: No, you are going in the wrong direction.

c) Q: I would like a room for one night, please.
A: One way or return?

d) Q: Is this the right bus to the theatre?
A: Certainly, we will be there in about ten minutes.

e) Q: Could you take me to Harvey Street quickly?
A: Would you like it with or without bathroom?

Other Places / Andere Orte

272 **Fill in the gaps. / Ergänzen Sie die Lücken.**

a) Peking is the ________________ of China.
b) The Atlantic is an ________________ .
c) Antarctica is the southernmost ________________ on earth.
d) The Alps are a ________________ in Europe.
e) Cuba is an ________________ in the Atlantic.
f) The Mississippi is the longest ________________ in North America.
g) The Aborigines are the ________________ of Australia.

273 **What is an *inhabitant*? / Was ist ein *inhabitant*?**

a) Staatsbürger/in ☐
b) Einwohner/in ☐
c) Mitbewohner/in ☐
d) Reisende/r ☐

274 **What do you call a person from these countries? / Wie heißt ein Mensch aus diesen Ländern?**

a) Poland ________________
b) Canada ________________
c) Germany ________________
d) Belgium ________________
e) France ________________
f) The United States of America ________________

g) India ____________________

h) The Philippines ____________________

i) Scotland ____________________

j) New Zealand ____________________

k) The Czech Republic ____________________

l) Greece ____________________

Where do these people come from? / Aus welchem Land kommen diese Menschen? 275

a) a Mexican ____________________

b) a Dutchwoman ____________________

c) an Egyptian ____________________

d) a Spaniard ____________________

e) a Hungarian ____________________

f) an Italian ____________________

g) an Irishman ____________________

h) a Thai ____________________

i) a Turk ____________________

j) a Japanese ____________________

k) a Portuguese ____________________

Fill in the adjectives for the place of origin. / Fügen Sie ein Adjektiv für den Herkunftsort ein. 276

a) Gorgonzola is an ______________ cheese.

b) Cognac is a ______________ brandy.

c) Gandhi was an ______________ Prime Minister.

d) Togo is an ______________ country.

e) An Audi is a ______________ car.

f) A wok is a ______________ pot.

g) Zurich is a ______________ town.

h) Pushkin is a ______________ author.

i) A bagpipe is a ______________ instrument.

277 **Name the four points of the compass. / Nennen Sie die vier Himmelsrichtungen.**

_________________ _________________

_________________ _________________

278 **Fill in the adjective in the correct form. / Ergänzen Sie das Adjectiv in der richtigen Steigerungsform.**

a) A hill is ________ (small) than a mountain.
b) Asia is the ________ (big) continent on earth.
c) The Atlantic is ________ (cold) than the Indian Ocean.
d) The culture of China is ________ (old) than the culture of Germany.
e) Kilimanjaro is the ________ (high) mountain in Africa.
f) Death Valley is the ________ (dry) place on earth.

279 **Connect the two right parts of these words. / Verbinden Sie die zwei richtigen Teile dieser Worte.**

a) rain	– side
b) land	tide
c) hill	Pole
d) high	– shore
e) sun	– scape
f) earth	– rise
g) sea	– forest
h) South	– quake

280 **Connect the word with its definition. / Verbinden Sie das Wort mit seiner Bedeutung.**

a) a volcano	a place where water comes out of the ground
b) a tributary	a very wet area of wasteland
c) a peak	a mountain that issues smoke and fire
d) a beach	the place where the land meets the sea
e) a spring	a river that joins a bigger river or a lake
f) a moor	the highest point on a mountain

Fill in the English word. / Ergänzen Sie das englische Wort. 281

a) Tibet was the __________ (interessanteste) country she visited.

b) The Freiburg cathedral is the __________ (schönste) church in the world.

c) Our holiday was __________ (langweiliger) than a weekend at home.

d) In the jungle the air is __________ (feuchter) than in the steppes.

e) He found it __________ (schwieriger) to learn Swahili than Dutch.

f) Passengers usually are __________ (am nervösten) during take-off.

g) Tony was never __________ (ängstlicher) than when he walked through a park at night.

Which language do they speak? / Welche Sprache sprechen sie? 282

a) The people in Turkey speak ________________ .

b) The people in Portugal speak ________________ .

c) The people in Norway speak ________________ .

d) The people in Finland speak ________________ .

e) The people in Sweden speak ________________ .

f) The people in England speak ________________ .

g) The people in France speak ________________ .

h) The people in Hungary speak ________________ .

i) The people in Denmark speak ________________ .

j) The people in Greece speak ________________ .

k) The people in Iceland speak ________________ .

l) The people in Kashmir speak ________________ .

m) The people in Persia speak ________________ .

n) The people in Catalonia speak ________________ .

o) The people in Slovakia speak ________________ .

Fill in the gaps. / Ergänzen Sie die Lücken. 283

national monument   scenery   ruin   game reserve   safari   tides

a) From the hotel window she saw the beautiful __________ of hills and villages.

b) The most famous __________ in Paris is the Eiffel Tower.

c) The height of the __________ depends on the phases of the moon.

d) A small chapel was built inside the __________ of the destroyed church.

e) Susan's photo-__________ went through six African countries.

f) A sturdy electric fence kept all the animals inside the __________ .

284 **Arrange from smallest to biggest. / Ordnen Sie diese Dinge vom kleinsten zum größten.**

a) hill, stone, rock, pebble, mountain

____

b) river, brook, rivulet

____

c) ocean, lake, sea, pond

____

d) wind, breeze, hurricane, gale, storm

____

285 **Name an antonym for the marked words. / Nennen Sie ein Antonym für die markierten Wörter.**

a) a **steep** slope __________

b) a **narrow** canyon __________

c) a **shallow** lake __________

d) a **high** mountain __________

e) a **long** walk __________

f) a **dangerous** journey __________

286 **Which sentence has a different meaning? / Welcher Satz bedeutet etwas anderes?**

a) The skyline of New York City moves from year to year. ☐

b) The skyline of New York City alters from year to year. ☐

c) The skyline of New York City changes from year to year. ☐

d) The skyline of New York City transforms from year to year. ☐

e) The skyline of New York City is modified from year to year. ☐

Which word does not fit? / Welches Wort paßt nicht? 287

a) height, pleasure, delight, enjoyment, fun, joy ______

b) to destroy, to check, to ruin, to wreck, to annihilate ______

c) sure, certain, definite, positive, valuable ______

d) to cry, to weep, to scream, to sob, to bawl ______

Derive adjectives from these verbs. /Bilden Sie aus diesen Verben Adjektive. 288

a) a friend who **helps** is a ______ friend

b) a car that **cannot be used** is a ______ car

c) a dog that wants to **sleep** is a ______ dog

d) a book that is **easy to read** is a ______ book

e) a number that **can be counted** is a ______ number

History and Politics / Geschichte und Politik

What is the person called? / Wie wird die Person genannt? 289

a) the leader of a tyranny ______

b) somebody who takes refuge ______

c) a member of a legislative body ______

d) somebody employed in diplomacy ______

e) somebody who conspires against something ______

f) somebody who engages in a revolution ______

g) somebody who takes part in a rebellion ______

h) somebody who represents the people ______

i) somebody who votes for something ______

What is it in English? / Wie heißt es auf englisch? 290

a) Regierung ______

b) Kabinett ______

c) Ministerpräsident/in ______

d) Kanzler/in ____________________

e) eine Wahl ____________________

f) Ministerium ____________________

g) eine Partei ____________________

291 **Complete the sentences. / Ergänzen Sie die Sätze.**

to the best of my memory *in our times* *at various times* *down the ages* *a sign of the times*

a) Humankind has lived in groups ___________ (durch alle Zeiten).

b) This area was overrun by the Huns ___________ (zu verschiedenen Zeiten) in history.

c) The increase of urban violence is ___________ (ein Zeichen der Zeit).

d) ___________ (soweit ich mich erinnere) Sir Walter Raleigh was executed.

e) To most people ___________ (in unserer Zeit) success is important.

292 **Fill in the gaps. / Ergänzen Sie die Sätze.**

formed *held* *entered* *called* *adjourned* *overthrow* *discussed*

a) The revolutionaries planned to ___________ (stürzen) the government.

b) Tom ___________ (beitreten) the Socialist Party at the age of twenty.

c) The Premier ___________ (einberufen) a cabinet meeting.

d) They ___________ (diskutieren) ways to combat unemployment.

e) The winning party ___________ (bilden) a new government.

f) At eleven p.m. the meeting was ___________ (vertagen).

g) The union ___________ (abhalten) a demonstration against wage cuts.

293 **Which sentence is right? / Welcher Satz stimmt?**

a) This is the first time a woman was made as Minister of Defence. ☐

b) This is the first time a woman was appointed as Minister of Defence. ☐

c) This is the first time a woman was named as Minister of Defence. ☐

d) This is the first time a woman was called as Minister of Defence. ☐

Connect the word with its definition. / Verbinden Sie das Wort mit seiner Bedeutung. 294

a) to conspire	to resist somebody in an argument
b) conviction	to secretly plan an unlawful act
c) constituency	to declare that something is wrong and punishable
d) to contradict	a group of citizens allowed to elect a representative
e) to condemn	a strong belief

Which sentences are right? / Welche Sätze sind richtig? 295

a) She did not share his sights on politics. ☐
b) She did not share his views on politics. ☐
c) She did not share his meaning on politics. ☐
d) She did not share his opinion on politics. ☐

Complete the following titles. / Ergänzen Sie die Titel. 296

a) __________ of Government	Regierungschef(in)
b) __________ Officer	Gemeindebeamte(r)
c) __________ President	Vizepräsident(in)
d) Ministry of __________	Handelsministerium
e) Secretary of __________	US Außenminister(in)
f) Ministry of __________	UK Innenministerium

Connect the halves. / Verbinden sie die passenden Satzhälften. 297

a) to levy	the throne
b) to adopt	a medal
c) to mount	a resolution
d) to crush	an uprising
e) to confer	a vote
f) to elect to	taxes
g) to cast	an office

298 **Which is not a definition of *constitution*? / Was ist keine Definition von *constitution?***

a) an established law or custom ☐
b) the physical makeup of an individual ☐
c) the process of uniting two or more groups ☐
d) the structure of something ☐

299 **Fill in the gaps. / Ergänzen Sie die Lücken.**

subjects realm ballot sovereign nobility

a) The citizens voted for a new president by secret ____________ .
b) Only the members of the ____________ attended the coronation.
c) The king's loyal ____________ honoured and adored him.
d) Napoleon was ____________ of several countries.
e) The Spanish ____________ once extended into Africa.

300 **Which word does not fit? / Welches Wort paßt nicht?**

a) dictatorship, democracy, society, confederation, monarchy
b) aristocrat, monarch, salary, dynasty, nobility
c) resign, abdicate, dethrone, retire, appoint

301 **What is the English word for *verklagen*? / Was heißt *verklagen* auf englisch?**

a) to convict ☐
b) to sentence ☐
c) to sue ☐
d) to prosecute ☐

302 **Name the epoch in history. / Nennen Sie die geschichtliche Epoche.**

Stone Age Renaissance Middle Ages modern times

a) The witch hunts took place in the ________________ .
b) The humanistic revival started in the ________________ .
c) The two world wars took place in ________________ .
d) Humankind used tools of stone in the ________________ .

Derive nouns from these words. / Bilden Sie Hauptwörter. 303

a) conclude ____________________

b) weak ____________________

c) meet ____________________

d) secure ____________________

Give an antonym for the following words. / Nennen Sie ein Antonym für jedes Wort. 304

a) powerful ____________________

b) social ____________________

c) responsible ____________________

d) kind ____________________

What is a *lawsuit*? / Was ist ein *lawsuit*? 305

a) the special clothing that judges wear ☐

b) a process by which one seeks justice in a court ☐

c) a high degree of punishment ☐

d) somebody who gives the law to the people ☐

Derive nouns from these words. / Bilden Sie aus diesen Wörtern Hauptwörter. 306

a) good ____________________

b) long ____________________

c) govern ____________________

d) wide ____________________

e) continue ____________________

Choose the right word. / Wählen Sie das richtige Wort. 307

a) Several **lands/countries** boycotted the international sports event.

b) The law states that all children must **attend/visit** school.

c) The American and the Japanese **company/society** have very different views on the role of women.

d) The opposition **won/one** the election in a landslide.

308 **Fill in the word *limit*, *border* or *frontier*. / Fügen Sie *limit*, *border* oder *frontier* ein.**

a) My patience has reached its ___________.

b) Some ___________ towns in the plains were attacked by Indians.

c) A customs officer checks your passport at the ___________ between two countries.

d) There seems to be no ___________ to the amount Cathy can eat.

309 **What is not a definition of *governor*? / Was ist keine Definition von *governor*?**

a) an official that rules over an area ☐

b) the director of an organisation ☐

c) a professional historian ☐

d) a slang word for a man who has some authority ☐

The Arts / Die Schönen Künste

310 **Which instrument is it?/ Nennen Sie das Musikinstrument.**

a) It has black and white keys. _____________

b) It is very large and most churches have one. _____________

c) It is the traditional instrument of Scotland. _____________

d) It has strings and it is important in rock music. _____________

e) It was used to play fanfares to announce kings. _____________

f) One bangs them together to make a sound. _____________

g) The angels play them in heaven. _____________

311 **Complete the questions. / Ergänzen Sie die Fragen.**

a) Q: What ______ ______ ________ do you like?

A: I like jazz and rock music.

b) Q: Do you ______ ______ ________ ?

A: Yes, I play the drums.

Fill in the gaps. / Ergänzen Sie diese Sätze. 312

accompanied favourite venues tuned up

a) My ____________ kind of music is opera.

b) The orchestra ____________ their instruments just before the concert started.

c) A newcomer ____________ the diva on the piano.

d) The pop group played at eleven ____________ in Germany.

What is it in English? / Wie heißt es auf englisch? 313

a) Zugabe ____________

b) die Streicher ____________

c) vorsingen/vorspielen ____________

d) Kammermusik ____________

e) die Tonleiter ____________

f) Dur ____________

g) Moll ____________

Fill in the gaps. / Ergänzen Sie die Lücken. 314

interpretation performance took their bows ovation

After one month of intense rehearsing, the orchestra was ready to give a ________________ . They played an unusually modern ________________ of Beethoven's Ninth Symphony.

The audience was delighted by it and gave a standing ____________ . When the soloists ______________ many listeners threw flowers onto the stage.

Which musician uses these objects to make music? / Wer macht mit diesen Dingen Musik? 315

a) the voice ____________

b) sticks ____________

c) a bow ____________

d) a baton ____________

316 **Give an antonym for each word. / Nennen Sie jeweils ein Antonym.**

a) sensitive ______________

b) experienced ______________

c) careful ______________

d) generous ______________

317 **What is a *recorder*? Was ist ein *recorder*?**

a) a disk with grooves that reproduces sound ☐

b) a wind instrument made of wood with eight finger holes ☐

c) a person who manages the schedule of an orchestra ☐

318 **Do you recognise these musical instruments? / Erkennen Sie die Instrumente?**

a) ndagr nopia ______________ the largest type of piano

b) netatscas ______________ a small rhythm instrument used in flamenco

c) jonab ______________ the string instrument used in American country music

d) sristng ______________ the stringed instruments of an orchestra

e) onexosaph ______________ the curved wind instrument used in jazz

319 **Nine instruments are hidden here. Can you find them? / Erkennen Sie die neun Instrumente, die hier versteckt sind?**

d	e	a	f	e	n	h	o	o	p	s
r	e	s	t	p	i	a	n	o	e	l
u	t	r	a	n	n	r	u	g	m	b
m	s	t	r	u	m	p	e	t	j	a
s	d	o	c	k	s	s	g	i	t	n
e	e	v	i	o	l	i	n	l	e	j
p	e	t	t	y	s	c	e	l	l	o
h	s	o	t	m	p	h	n	r	u	f
e	o	p	i	e	f	o	o	u	y	e
j	e	r	c	l	a	r	i	n	e	t
d	o	n	n	i	k	d	g	o	o	m

What is not a definition of *note*? / Was ist keine Definition von *note*? 320

a) a characteristic feature ☐

b) a symbol used for writing music ☐

c) a piece of paper money ☐

d) the thumb hole of a wind instrument ☐

Which word does not rhyme? / Welches Wort reimt nicht? 321

a) hymn, pilgrim, minim, him, thyme, rhythm

b) violin, engine, combine, origin, emotion, foreign

c) pure, tour, endure, newer, epicure, moor, choir

d) staff, calf, rough, carafe, giraffe, laugh

Fill in the prepositions. / Ergänzen Sie die Präpositionen. 322

a) „Let It Be“ is a famous song ________ the Beatles.

b) Louis Armstrong lived ________ Ludwig van Beethoven.

c) Sarah loves to dance ________ waltzes by Johann Strauß.

d) The saxophone is an important instrument ________ jazz.

e) Helen listened to a concert ________ the radio.

Connect the English and the German. / Verbinden Sie das Deutsche mit dem Englischen. 323

a) to sight-read music	verstimmt sein
b) to tune an instrument	zu tief sein
c) to be flat	Musik vom Blatt spielen
d) to be out of tune	den Grundton angeben
e) to play by heart	ein Instrument stimmen
f) to give the keynote	auswendig spielen

What do the following idioms mean? / Was bedeuten diese Redewendungen? 324

a) to play second fiddle

____

b) for a song

____

c) to make a song about something

____

d) to play it by ear

____

325 **What is a *novel*? / Was ist eine *novel*?**

a) a brand-new book ☐
b) a very long prose story ☐
c) a place that exists only in the imagination ☐

326 **Which sentence asks for one special edition? / In welchem Satz wird nach einer Ausgabe gefragt?**

a) I need a piece of the Riverside Shakespeare. ☐
b) I need an example of the Riverside Shakespeare. ☐
c) I need a copy of the Riverside Shakespeare. ☐
d) I need an outpost of the Riverside Shakespeare. ☐

327 **Translate the following. / Übersetzen Sie folgendes.**

a) a poem ____________________
b) a line ____________________
c) a paragraph ____________________
d) a chapter ____________________
e) a volume ____________________

328 **Fill in the gaps. / Ergänzen Sie die Lücken.**

play *nursery rhymes* *diary* *non-fiction* *review*

a) Anne Frank wrote down her daily experiences in a ________________ .
b) At ten a.m. every day new books are presented in a book ________________ on the radio.
c) Is “Hamlet” or “Romeo and Juliet” the most famous ________________ by Shakespeare?

d) Do-it-yourself manuals head the _______________ best-seller list.

e) _______________ are simple little poems for children.

Connect the English and the German. / Verbinden Sie das Deutsche mit dem Englischen. 329

a) an abridged encyclop(a)edia	eine Zusammenfassung der Handlung
b) the gist of the talk was clear	ein gekürztes Lexikon
c) engravings illustrated the poems	die Hauptaussage war deutlich
d) a summary of the plot	Stiche stellte die Gedichte dar

Which artists create these works? / Welche Künstler schaffen diese Werke? 330

a) a painting _______________

b) a sculpture _______________

c) a sonata _______________

d) a poem _______________

Fill in the gaps. / Ergänzen Sie die Lücken. 331

box-office *playbill* *cloak room* *part/role*

a) Tickets for the performance were on sale at the _______________ .

b) We left our coats in the _______________ .

c) Julie bought a _______________ with information about the play.

d) The star's first _______________ had been Ophelia in her school play.

Complete the idioms with phrases with *put*. / Ergänzen Sie diese idiomatischen Ausdrücke mit Phrasen mit *put*. 332

putting on *put my finger on it* *put words into my mouth* *put his foot into it*

a) Don't _______________ (misquote me). I did not say that.

b) Our local theatre is _______________ (showing) two operas.

c) He really _______________ (made a mistake) when he thought that she was older.

d) Something is wrong, but I can't ______________________ (say exactly what it is).

333 **What are the *acts* of a play? / Was sind die *acts* eines Schauspiels?**

a) die Besetzung der Schauspieler/innen ☐

b) die Nacktszenen im Stück ☐

c) die großen Handlungsabschnitte ☐

d) das Bühnenbild ☐

Solutions / Lösungen

Introductions / Sich vorstellen

1 Hello. I am your new vocabulary trainer. I am still **quite** young and you are one **of** my first readers.
I was born in the year 1996 into a large and **well-known** family of educational books. My ancestors are successful dictionaries, grammar books and works of reference. Our **place of birth** is the city of Munich. However, you can **meet** us in very **many** places **in** Europe and sometimes on other continents.
I am pleased to have **met** you and I am looking **forward to** working with you.

2 a) *Good Luck!* ist keine Begrüßung
b) *yours affectionately* ist eine Schlußformel für Briefe

3 A president - Good morning, Madam/Sir.
A good friend - There you are, old chum!
The Pope - Good evening, Your Holiness.
Your husband - Hello, Love!
Your baby daughter - Hi, Honey!
A queen - Good evening, Your Highness.
Your boss - Good morning, Madam/Sir.

4 a) name b) sure c) familiar d) recognise

5 b) You remind me of the actress from the movie "Dr. Shivago".

Merke:
to remind somebody of something heißt *jemanden an etwas erinnern, remember* bedeutet *sich an etwas erinnern,* und *recognise* heißt *erkennen*.

6 a) What is your name?
b) Where were you born?
c) Who are your parents?
d) When are you planning to arrive?

7 Hallo, Karen. May I **introduce** you to my husband Frank? I don´t think the two of you have **met** before. Frank, this **is** my old friend Karen. Karen, this **is** Frank.
Frank and I first **noticed** each other at my brother´s birthday party even though we had been **living** in the same street for two years. We did not **know** that we were almost neighbours.

8 How do you do? I am pleased to meet you. It was lovely seeing you again. I hope we will meet again soon! How are you today?

9 a) to visit somebody b) to insult somebody c) to give up part of one's opinion in order to come to an agreement d) to be unlucky

10 **This**, right here, is my colleague Edna. Standing **next** to her is her boyfriend Sven.

The woman **behind,** not in front of the little table, is my sister Andrea and the couple sitting **on** the couch are my parents.

11 Fine, thanks. - Gut, danke. So-so. - Es geht so. Can't complain. - Kann nicht klagen. Very well, thank you. - Sehr gut, danke! Down in the dumps. - Miserabel.

12 a) I've come to say **good-bye.**
b) What time are you **leaving**?
c) My train **leaves** at 6 p.m.
d) I have **called** a taxi for 5.30 p.m.

13 b) Please, give my regards to your mother.

Merke:
Jemanden grüßen heißt *give my regards to ...*, *der Gruß* hingegen ist *a greeting*.

14

Would you like to have a drink with me?	Yes, I would very much like to.
It's been lovely talking to you.	Thank you, I also enjoyed our conversation.
Shall we meet tomorrow evening?	I'm sorry, I can't. I'm busy tomorrow.
Would you like to go to a pub?	I would prefer to go to a café.
When can we meet again?	I would rather not see you again.

Family and Friends / Familie und Freunde

15 a) nephew b) father c) grandfather d) cousin e) granddaughter

16

17 a) stepfather b) stepsister c) half-brother d) son-in-law

18 a) **home** - ist keine Verwandtschaftsbezeichnung
b) **independence day** - ist kein Familienereignis
c) **cousin** - kann Cousin und Cousine bezeichnen

19 Every two years all the members of our family gather for a **family reunion**. My parents, my brothers and sisters, and all my cousins come. Some of our common **ancestors** come from the 18th century. All the relatives not related by blood are my **in-laws.**

At the reunions we enjoy talking about our long **lineage**. We all descend from a large farm, our original **family seat** in the Black Forest.

20 a) wrong: husband, should be wife
b) wrong: enemy, should be friend
c) wrong: youngest, should be oldest
d) wrong: adolescent, should be adult

21 a) as deaf as a post
b) as blind as a bat
c) as strong as a horse
d) as hard as nails
e) as pretty as a picture

Jobs and Professions / Arbeit und Beruf

22 Paul Bocuse → cook, Marlene Dietrich → actress, Indira Ghandi → president, John Lennon → singer / song writer, Sherlock Holmes → detective, Vincent van Gogh → painter / artist, Confucius → philosopher, Franz Beckenbauer → sportsman, coach, Madame Curie → chemist, inventress, Maria Callas → opera singer

23 a) a **freelance** reporter b) in the medical **profession** c) a **staff** of only 14 people d) held many **jobs** e) is a **retiree** f) a **civil servant** g) my **daily duties** include

24 actor → actress, monk → nun, tailor → seamstress, sales clerk → sales clerk, headmaster → headmistress, waiter → waitress, policeman → policewoman, priest → priestess, poet → poetess, emperor → empress

Merke:
Viele englische Berufsbezeichnungen verweisen nicht auf ein bestimmtes Geschlecht, z.B. *electrician, dancer, teacher*. Unterschiede zwischen der männlichen und weiblichen Form werden oft mit der Nachsilbe *-ess* für die weiblich Form gekennzeichnet. In vielen Fällen sind die männliche und weibliche Form aber auch verschiedene Wörter.

25 a) job → a specific duty b) profession → requires special knowledge and often academic training c) labour → a physical or mental activity that requires much effort d) occupation → the principal business of one's life e) work → a physical or mental activity

26 c) a responsible position at one's workplace

27 a) discoverer b) composer c) inventor d) creator

28 a) only one **worked** b) she **worked off** her anger c) The volume can be **worked out** d) They had **worked out** a clever scheme e) He was all **worked up**

29 a) an electrician b) a judge c) a minister, a priest d) a doctor, a physician e) a fireman/firewoman f) a dentist g) a carpenter h) an author i) a teacher

30 c) How does it work? bedeutet *Wie geht das?*

> **Merke:**
> What do you do for living? What is your line of work? What is your occupation heißt: *Was sind Sie von Beruf?*

31 a) white collar worker b) apprentice c) skilled workers d) craftswoman

32 a) apprentice, skilled worker, foreman, manager, director
b) pupil, teacher, principal, minister of education
c) baby, toddler, adolescent, adult, senior citizen
d) acolyte, priest, bishop, archbishop, pope
e) knight, duke, queen, empress

33 a) tailor/tailoress b) mechanic c) secretary d) sailor e) sculptor/sculptress f) baker g) policeman/policewoman h) bank clerk i) doctor, physician j) hairdresser, barber

34 a) wage b) salary c) pay

> **Merke:**
> *Wage* bezieht sich auf den Lohn, den Arbeiter bekommen, und wird in der Regel wöchentlich bezahlt. *A salary* ist ein Gehalt, das meistens monatlich bezahlt wird. *Pay* ist ein informeller Begriff, der Löhne aller Art bezeichnet.

35 c) I work promotion ist falsch, richtig wäre „I have been promoted."

36 a) on holiday b) at work c) in the sales department d) for a new job

37 a) shares b) entrepreneur c) monopoly d) stock market e) union f) headquarters

38 a) There's honour among thieves. → Eine Krähe hackt der anderen kein Auge aus.
b) To be as mad as a hatter. → Eine Meise unterm Hut haben.
c) To cut one's coat according to one's cloth. → Sich nach der Decke strecken.
d) To put one's nose to the grindstone. → Ranklotzen.
e) To be a smooth customer. → Ein ganz geriebener Kerl sein.

At School / In der Schule

39 a) nursery school (UK), kindergarten (US) b) elementary school (US), primary school (UK) c) university d) pupil (UK), student (US) e) scholar

40 b) There was not one flaw in Marion's excellent spelling test.
c) There was not one blunder in Marion's excellent spelling test.
d) There was not one fault in Marion's excellent spelling test.

> **Merke:**
> Die Wörter *mistake, flaw, blunder, fault, error* haben zwar alle die Bedeutung *Fehler*, es gibt jedoch folgende Unterschiede: *fault* und *flaw* bezeichnen meistens eine Beeinträchtigung der Funktion, während *blunder* eine grobe Fehleinschätzung in Situationen des gesellschaftlichen Lebens bezeichnet.

41 a) subject b) blackboard c) extra curricular d) library e) auditorium

42

P	E	N	S	T	**M**	O	**M**	O	U	R
L	**I**	**T**	**E**	**R**	**A**	**T**	**U**	**R**	**E**	I
A	**G**	I	N	G	**T**	T	**S**	U	G	H
N	**R**	**E**	K	**A**	**H**	E	**I**	P	A	G
E	**A**	D	**O**	**L**	**S**	T	**C**	H	**H**	A
T	**M**	Z	U	**G**	D	O	L	E	**I**	M
E	**M**	O	G	**E**	**R**	S	A	P	**S**	E
A	**A**	M	P	**B**	E	**A**	T	O	**T**	A
S	**R**	I	C	**R**	A	T	**P**	L	**O**	T
G	**Y**	**M**	X	**A**	**R**	**T**	I	**H**	**R**	I
A	**C**	**H**	**E**	**M**	**I**	**S**	**T**	**R**	**Y**	E

43 a) literature b) history c) geometry d) geography e) grammar f) biology

44 a) fail b) lazy c) slow d) untidy e) late

45 a) counsellor b) librarian c) coach d) choir master/mistress e) principal (US), headmaster/headmistress (UK)

46 Before school starts in the morning, all the children lock their coats and their school bags in their **lockers**. When the **bell** rings they hurry to their **classrooms**.
In some rooms the children sit at normal tables, but most classrooms have proper school **desks**.
If a teacher **returns** a test that was written the day before, the children are very curious about everybody's **grade/result**.
There is a long **recess** in the middle of the school day with enough time to eat a **packed lunch** and play in the **playground (US)**, **schoolyard (UK)**.
On special occasions the pupils and the teachers **assemble** in the auditorium before they go home and listen to the principal make **announcements**.

47 a) the orchestra **took up** practising
b) the pupils **took turns** hitting
c) the explosion ... **took** them all **by surprise**
d) children **take** ... schools **for granted**
e) „Tom Sawyer" **took** my grandfather **back**
f) to **take** an engine **to pieces**
g) **took** no **notice** of

48 a) *completion* ist keine schulische Beurteilung b) *demonstrate* bedeutet nicht *prüfen* c) *copy* heißt *nachahmen* und muß sich nicht auf die Malerei beziehen d) *timid* bedeuted *ängstlich* e) *abstract* heißt nicht *erfinderisch* f) *interrogate* heißt *vernehmen*, nicht *sprechen/vortragen.*

49 a) in b) on c) at d) in/of d) after

50 a) teacher b) tutor c) lecturer d) instructor

51 a) indetermination, hesitation b) eager, enthusiastic, avid, fervent c) unite, ally, associate, join d) impede, hinder, prevent, deter e) deteriorate, worsen f) conceit, ambition, immodesty, grandeur g) immoderate, extreme, excessive, extravagant

52 a) a fountain pen b) an eraser (US), a rubber (UK) c) a ruler d) a dictionary e) a school uniform

53 c) marked by respect and consideration for others

54 a) he is really only half-baked b) like two peas in a pod c) two-faced d) three sheets to the wind e) to have his forty winks f) on its last leg g) the last straw

In the City / In der Stadt

55 a) a monastery b) a palace c) an orphanage d) a hotel e) an old age home f) a hospital

56 a) way b) nearest c) area d) direction e) one-way

57 c) a place where pupils live if their home is far from school

58
a) cottage, house, mansion, palace
b) hamlet, village, town, city
c) path, alley, street, highway
d) chamber, room, suite, building

59 a) church b) bell tower c) cathedrals d) chapel e) synagogue f) mosque g) temples

60 a) a pedestrian b) an intersection c) a zebra crossing d) street/road signs e) traffic lights (US), robot (UK) f) a cyclist g) a conductor h) a sidewalk (US), a pavement (UK) i) a street vendor j) a parking meter

61 My uncle Bernie lives in one of the many **suburbs** that surround Chicago. There, he owns the right half of a **semi-detached** house. Before his daughter Cathy moved into the other half, she had rented a flat in a large **apartment building** in the middle of Chicago.

Cathy finally moved out of the **inner city** because she felt threatened by the gangs that roamed her **neighbourhood**. Now, she misses the view of the Sears Tower, the most famous **skyscraper** of Chicago - but she is glad that she can park her car right at her front door and no longer in an underground **parking garage.**

62 a) dairy b) bakery c) butcher's d) book shop (UK), book store (US) e) newsagent's f) stationery shop/store g) hardware shop/store h) chemist's, pharmacy (UK), drugstore (US) i) ice cream parlo(u)r j) jeweller's h) travel agent/agency

63 a) city map b) station c) supermarket d) museum e) theatre f) pavilion g) pond

64 a) through b) to c) on d) next e) near f) in g) at h) by

65
a) a cottage is a building for people, all the other words mean buildings for equipment and/or animals
b) a direction is not a type of road
c) to run is to move very quickly, the other words mean to walk around without a goal
d) narrow means not wide, the other words mean very small
e) to devise is to invent or create, the other words mean to build

66 a) coarse or indelicate or simple b) construct or erect c) uncomplicated or plain or simple d) advanced or civilised e) repel or reject f) future or prospective

67 an apartment → a flat the ground floor → the bottom stor(e)y rest rooms → toilets, the loo a faucet → a tap an elevator → a lift a sidewalk → a pavement a parking structure → a parking garage a gas station → a petrol station the drugstore → the chemist's a subway → an underground a traffic light → a robot a store → a shop

68 a) gone off b) gone back on their promises c) gone to his head d) went from bad to worse e) gone out of business f) went haywire g) go round h) went over

69 c) The domestic language of Australia is English.

Merke:
Domestic hat folgende Bedeutungen: 1. zum Haushalt oder der Familie gehörend, 2. zum eigenen Land gehörend, nicht fremd sein.
In Verbindung mit *language* werden jedoch die Adjektive *native* oder *national* benutzt.

At Home / Zu Hause

70 a) lounge/living room b) kitchen c) study d) bathroom e) pantry f) nursery g) attic h) cellar (UK), basement (US)

71 a) a gable b) a chimney c) a fireplace d) a staircase, a stairwell, stairs e) bricks f) a balcony g) a veranda h) shutters

72 d) bedroom

Merke:
rest room ist ein Raum, meistens in öffentlichen Gebäuden, für den privaten Rückzug mit Waschgelegenheiten und Toilette.

73 a) portal → a grand and imposing entrance b) threshold → the plank or stone that lies under a door c) entrance → the place or the act of entry d) gate → an opening in a wall or fence e) door → a swinging or sliding barrier that closes an entry f) porch → a roofed entrance to a building

74 a) a spoon b) a bread knife c) a whisk d) a sheet e) a curtain f) a broom g) a wardrobe, a cupboard, a closet (US) h) a cork screw i) a bottle opener j) a tin opener (UK), a can opener (US) k) a match, a lighter

75 a) Joe's house was not harmed by the tornado.
c) Joe's house was not damaged by the tornado.

Merke:
Mit *damage* werden Schäden an Dingen ausgedrückt, *injure* und *hurt* beziehen sich dagegen auf Menschen und Tiere. *Harm* bezieht sich auf Dinge und Lebewesen.

76 cups and saucers, knives and forks, salt and pepper, pillow and blanket, tables and chairs, shoes and socks, plug and socket

77 a) to do the laundry b) to do the dishes c) to dry the dishes d) to draw the curtains e) to switch/turn on the light f) to watch television g) to turn down the volume h) to answer the phone i) to make coffee j) to light a candle k) to extinguish a candle

78 a) bedding b) furniture c) cutlery d) tools

79 a) wallpaper b) light bulb c) eiderdown (UK), comforter (US) d) sink e) socket

80 a) a high chair b) a love seat c) a bench d) an arm chair e) a sofa f) a rocking chair g) a deck chair h) a throne

81 a) already b) still c) yet d) already e) still f) yet

Merke:
Still wird für Tätigkeiten benutzt, die in der Gegenwart geschehen, *yet* meistens bei Fragen oder Verneinungen. *Already* heißt *schon* oder *bereits* und bezieht sich auf etwas, das in der Vergangenheit geschehen ist.

82 a) house b) home c) dwellings d) residence

Merke:
House bezieht sich ausschließlich auf Einfamilienhäuser. *Home* deutet eine enge emotionale Beziehung zwischen Mensch und Haus an. *Dwelling* ist viel abstrakter und deutet keine solche Beziehung an. *Residence* gehört zur gehobenen Sprache.

83 a) **wage** hat nichts mit dem Mietgeschäft zu tun
b) **line** ist eine *Linie*, nicht unbedingt eine Grenze
c) **produce** heißt nicht *zahlen*, sondern *erschaffen*
d) **pointed** heißt *spitz*, alle anderen bedeuten *hoch*

84 a) landlord/landlady b) rent c) drive (UK), driveway (US) d) fence

85 a) a toaster b) a coffee machine c) a blow dryer d) a dishwasher e) a washing machine f) a dryer g) a vacuum cleaner h) a lawnmower

86 b) Alan takes a shower every morning.

87 James and Sally spent many hours redecorating their bathroom. They had to lay new **pipes** because they changed the position of the **plumbing fixtures**. They put new **tiles** on the walls and installed two **basins** because they want to get ready at the same time every morning. They covered the wall above the basins with a large **mirror** made of Italian glass.
Since both like to relax in hot water after work, they chose an especially comfortable **bath(tub)**, but they also built in a **shower** for quick refreshing in the mornings.

Merke:
Bath bezeichnet im amerikanischen Englisch eine Badewanne, im britischen jedoch das Badezimmer. Ein Badezimmer heißt in Amerika ***bathroom,*** die Badewanne in Großbritannien ***bathtub*** oder nur ***tub***.

88 duschen → to take a shower, baden → to take a bath, Zähne putzen → to brush one's teeth, sich schminken → to put on make up, Haare kämmen → to comb one's hair, Füße schrubben → to scrub one's feet, Nägel schneiden → to cut one's nails, Haare föhnen → to blow-dry one's hair, Schnürsenkel zubinden → to tie ones (shoe)laces, Mantel zuknöpfen → to button (up) one's coat, Mantel aufknöpfen → to unbutton one's coat

89 a) on b) on c) of d) in e) to f) on g) off h) on i) on

90 To pull the wool over somebody's eyes. → Jemandem Sand in die Augen streuen. To take somebody for a ride. → Jemand übers Ohr hauen. To have a finger in the pie. → Eine Hand im Spiel haben. To show one's true colours. → Sein/Ihr wahres Gesicht zeigen. To win hands down. → Mit links gewinnen. To be up to every trick. → Mit allen Wassern gewaschen sein.

91 a) a good dinner b) plays well c) a good hostess d) Mash well! e) decorated well

Merke:
Good ist ein Adjektiv und wird benutzt, um Substantive oder Pronomen zu beschreiben. *Well* ist ein Adverb und wird benutzt, um Verben, Adjektive oder andere Adverbien genauer zu bestimmen.

Food, Clothing, Shopping / Lebensmittel, Kleidung, Einkaufen

92 a) breakfast b) a packed lunch c) lunch d) afternoon tea e) supper f) dinner g) picnic

93 a) I am thirsty. b) I quench my thirst. c) They are hungry. d) They appease their hunger. e) They starve to death. / They are dying of hunger. f) She has a snack. g) That is her favourite dish.

94 a) Please set the table for supper. b) Dinner is served in five minutes. c) Do you take milk or sugar in your tea? d) Would you care for some more wine? e) You can clear the table when we're done. f) Let me help you with the dishes.

95 a) Tracy's parents **ate** at **eight** o'clock every evening. b) If you **meet** vegetarians, never offer them **meat**. c) After travelling in the **desert**, the tourists chose a cold **dessert**. d) There was no **peace** in the class until each child had a **piece** of cake. e) The secret **source** of the truffles in his **sauce** was somewhere in France. f) One **whole** cheese weighs very little because there are many **hole**s in it. g) You need a **pair** of **pear**s and three apples for this cake. h) Terrence could not **wait** to loose five pounds of **weight**.

96 champagne → bubbly, french fries → greasy, ice cream → cold, chocolate icing →

sweet, pickles → sour, chilli peppers → hot, apple pie → fruity, marshmallow → soft, coffee → strong, steak → rare

97 strawberry, raspberry, cranberry, boysenberry, blueberry, blackberry

98 a) artificial sweetener b) egg yolk c) ingredients d) carbonated e) brewery f) preservatives g) slices h) an onion

99 a) a *grape* is not a vegetable b) an *onion* is not a fruit c) a *nut* is not a herb d) to *bake* is not a method used to prepare eggs

100 a) poultry b) beef c) veal d) mutton e) pork f) venison

101 a) to season with salt and pepper b) to fold in egg white c) to whip cream d) to fry a steak e) to scramble eggs

102 Barbara is very choosy about her **nutrition**. That is why she bakes her own bread. She uses only whole wheat **flour** and other healthy **ingredients** for the dough. While the bread bakes in the oven a delicious **smell** permeates the whole house. It is a fine delicacy if you **spread** some butter on a fresh **slice** of Barbara's bread.

103 a) make out (understand) b) Make a stand (resist) c) make no secret of (don't conceal) d) Make the most of (exploit) e) made peace (ended hostilities) f) made things worse (worsened conditions)

104 a) Peter's chocolate cake tastes very good.
c) A cup of hot tea would feel good now.
f) Philip's writing has become good.

Merke:
Die Verben *be, become, grow, seem, appear, look, feel, taste, sound, smell* brauchen ein prädikatives Adjektiv, um das Subjekt zu beschreiben.

105 a) booked b) order c) decided d) recommend e) take f) are out of g) have h) enjoy

106 a) booking b) menu c) waitress d) order e) aperitif f) beverage g) main course

107 a) May I help you? b) We're sold out of cheddar. Would you like some gouda instead? c) How much is it?

108 a) an aisle b) a cash register c) a shopping cart (US), a trolley (UK) d) the change e) a discount f) a scale g) clearance sale

109 a) expensive b) light c) stale, old d) together e) loose f) smaller g) narrow h) old fashioned

110 a) suits (look good on) b) flattering (favourable) c) altered (changed) d) dry cleaned (chemically cleaned) e) dye (change the colour) f) matches (looks good with)

111 a) gloves b) socks c) a scarf d) a belt e) a bathing/swimming suit f) boots g) (silk) stockings h) a petticoat i) a suit j) a hat k) a tie l) an apron

112 a) cape b) belt c) hood d) tie e) fashion f) robe g) heels

113 a) size b) cut c) larger

114 c) The princess changes her clothes five times a day.

> **Merke:**
> *Sich umziehen* heißt *to change clothes, sich anziehen* heißt *to put on clothes.*

115
a) Tom opened his **umbrella** when it started to rain.
b) Grandmother's **glasses** slipped off her nose when she fell asleep.
c) Irene wiped her nose with a **handkerchief**.
d) Yvonne put on a woolen **sweater** when she was cold.
e) Emily put the golden **necklace** in her jewelry box.

> **Merke:**
> Es gibt die beiden Schreibweisen *jewelry* oder *jewellery.*

116

e	**p**	**y**	**j**	**a**	**m**	**a**	**s**	t	a	**c**
l	o	**e**	d	i	**p**	e	e	h	o	**a**
b	**e**	**l**	**t**	**s**	i	**a**	k	**h**	n	**r**
l	o	v	e	**t**	m	t	**n**	**a**	a	**d**
a	r	i	t	**o**	**i**	p	u	**t**	x	**i**
z	**i**	**p**	r	**c**	e	**c**	l	l	**s**	**g**
e	a	r	s	**k**	n	o	**o**	h	p	**a**
r	e	**s**	**k**	**i**	**r**	**t**	l	**a**	g	**n**
o	v	e	r	**n**	n	e	i	n	**t**	t
e	n	d	z	**g**	**l**	**o**	**v**	**e**	**s**	a
v	**e**	**i**	**l**	**s**	f	o	x	b	o	u

117 a) dress b) clothes c) clothing d) attire

> **Merke:**
> *Dress* bezeichnet hier das ganze Ensemble, das ein Mensch anhat. *Clothes* bezeichnet einzelne Kleidungsstücke, und *clothing* ist der Sammelbegriff für Kleidung. *Attire* und *apparel* sind Begriffe für sehr formelle Kleidung.

118 d) a pair of bras

119 c) He was looking for a correct pair of shoes for the wedding.

> **Merke:**
> *Suitable, fitting* und *appropriate* sind austauschbar und heißen alle *passend*. *Correct* heißt jedoch *richtig*.

120 b) Michael must clear his evening shoes before the ball.

121 a) wear b) worn c) waist d) sale e) heels

122 a) undressed b) dressed up c) got dressed d) dress e) dress

123 a) ran a temperature b) ran over c) ran across d) ran into a lot of difficulty e) ran out of f) time is running out g) on the run h) ran aground

The Time and Holidays / Zeitangaben, Festtage und Ferien

124 a) midnight b) leap year c) noon, midday d) daybreak e) night f) present

125 a) seasons b) century c) calender d) alarm clock e) holidays f) periods g) age

126 b) There is a full moon every 28 days.

127 a) current b) recently c) formerly d) in the future e) posterity f) at present g) now

128 a) Q: What is the time?
b) Q: What is the date, please?
c) Q: And which day of the week is it?
d) Q: Do you have/know the exact date?

129 a) winter b) autumn (UK), fall (US) c) summer d) spring e) Indian summer

130 a) slow b) fast c) goes off

131 a) a quarter past nine in the morning b) half past four in the afternoon c) five minutes past noon/twelve in the afternoon d) eight o'clock in the evening e) a quarter to twelve in the morning f) ten to eight in the evening g) almost six o'clock, one minute to six in the evening h) just past ten o'clock in the morning, two minutes past ten in the morning i) thirty-six minutes past eleven at night

> **Merke:**
> Das Wort *o'clock* wird in der Regel nur bei Nennung der vollen Stunde benutzt.

132 e) an artistic likeness or image

133 a) decade b) March c) month d) afternoon e) hourly f) second g) eleventh, twelfth h) Tuesday, Wednesday

> **Merke:**
> Wochentage und Monatsnamen werden im englischen, wie alle Eigennamen, großgeschrieben

134 a) lower b) trite c) quiet d) vow e) boomerang f) alone

135 a) delayed b) interval c) steady d) sudden e) temporary f) immediate g) simultaneously

136

a) ahead of time	früher als erwartet
b) before one's time	bevor jemand geboren wurde

c) Once upon a time — Es war einmal
d) to be pressed for time — sehr unter Zeitdruck stehen
e) to race against the time — im Wettlauf mit der Zeit
f) time after time — immer wieder
g) time out of mind — seit jeher

137 c) Their friendship lasted just one year.

Merke:
Last deutet an, daß eine Fortdauer begrenzt ist. *Persist* bezeichnet ein zwangsläufiges Fortbestehen, *continue* eine Fortdauer ohne Zeitbegrenzung. *Take* verweist auf eine benötigte Zeitspanne.

138 a) Easter b) New Year's Eve c) New Year's Day d) national holiday, Independence Day e) Christmas f) Valentine's Day g) wedding anniversary h) Halloween i) St. Patrick's Day

139 d) Charles visited many people to his wedding.

140 a) first b) third c) fifth d) thirty-first e) twentieth

141 a) until b) before c) on d) for e) at f) in g) at, on

Merke:
Die Präposition der Zeit *at* bezieht sich auf einen genauen Zeitpunkt oder auf Ferien-/Freizeiten. *On* verweist auf Tage, die Präposition *in* sowie *during* und *for* bezeichnen Zeitspannen.

142 a) always b) every c) never d) seldom e) ceaseless f) regularly

143 The fourth of July is the **national holiday** of the United States of America. Many special **events** take place on that day. If the weather is good, most Americans **celebrate** the day outside. Families will get together for an **outing** in the country or meet in a park to listen to one of the many **open air** concerts. The opera houses in the big cities present gala **performances** by famous singers and there are special **sports events** in the stadiums. When the **national anthem** is played at the beginning of the events the audience stands up respectfully. For most Americans the highlight of the day, however, are the spectacular **fireworks** that light up the night sky all over the country.

144 a) during b) strange c) finished d) get up e) end f) sky.

145 a) sad or melancholy or dejected b) unlucky or unfortunate or luckless c) boring or dull d) conflict ridden or quarrelsome e) together or gregarious f) loud or noisy or active

146 c) They want to go after Paris.

147 d) We long for a quiet hotel.

Merke:
To long for heißt *sich nach etwas sehnen.*

The Weather / Das Wetter

148 a) zero degrees b) the weather forecast c) the freezing point d) centigrade e) temperature f) air g) climate

149 a) a dewy early morning b) the scorching heat of the dog-days c) a raging hurricane d) the melting snow e) a keen frost f) glorious sunshine

150 a) weather map b) icicles c) avalanche d) lightning e) rainbow f) hailstones

151 b) The football match was cancelled due to heavy rainfall.

152 a) a peal of thunder b) a ray of sunshine c) a flash of lightning d) a gust of wind

153 a) dew b) overcast c) violent d) blond e) stride

154 a) frost b) blizzard c) earthquake d) flood e) drought

155 snowbank, snowball, snowblind, snowcap, snowdrift, snowfall, snowfield, snowflake, snowmaker, snowman, snowmelt, snowplow, snowshoe, snowslide, snowstorm, snowsuit, snowwoman

156 c) I have a cold.

> **Merke:**
> *I have a cold* heißt *Ich habe eine Erkältung*, alle anderen Sätze bedeuten *Ich friere*.

157 a) there b) day c) your d) deign e) can f) appetite g) stew

158 a) Ein Unglück kommt selten alleine. b) Es schüttet wie aus Kübeln. c) auf die hohe Kante legen d) ein Sturm im Wasserglas e) etwas spitzkriegen f) sehen, wie der Hase läuft g) unpäßlich, krank

159 rainbow, raincoat, raindrop, rainfall, rainproof, rainmaking, rainstorm, rainwater, rainwear

160
a) The ground was still **wet** after the rain.
b) The **billowing** wind blew off his hat.
c) The waves were very low in the **calm** ocean.
d) Vision was seriously limited on that **foggy** day.
e) April was marked by highly **changeable** weather - there was everything from glorious sunshine to severe snowstorms.
f) Not one ray of sun penetrated the **overcast** sky.

The Human Body / Der Mensch

161 a) eyes b) nose c) teeth d) brain e) hands f) posterior, buttocks, bottom g) back

162
a) What can I do for you?
b) Would you open your mouth, please?
c) Does it hurt if I press here?

d) Have you had trouble with it before?
e) Could you be pregnant?
f) How often does the pain come back?
g) Would you please rinse your mouth?

163 fingers, fingernails, toes, toenails

164 c) the arms and legs of a human being

165 a) respiration → Atmung b) appendix → Blinddarm c) calf → Wade d) bile → Galle e) temple → Schläfe f) kidney → Niere

166 a) pale b) pail c) way d) weigh e) waists f) waste g) wear h) carry

167 a) to pant, to gasp b) to stare c) to eavesdrop d) to squint e) to stutter f) to cling g) to limp, to stumble

168 a) pale b) ghost c) to lose one's senses d) reserved

Merke:
Das englische Wort *ghost* bedeutet in der Regel *Gespenst*. Das englische Wort für *Geist* im Sinne von *Seele* ist *spirit*.

169 c) He had very arrogant behaviour.

Merke:
Expression, *countenance* und *features* bedeuten alle *Gesichtsausdruck, behaviour* dagegen *Verhalten*. Ein weiteres Wort, das Wort *air,* kann sowohl den Gesichtsausdruck als auch die Gebärden beschreiben.

170 a) mute/dumb b) blind c) deaf d) numb e) lame, paralysed.

171 a) eyebrows b) eyelids c) eyelashes d) iris e) pupil f) blind spot

172 a) for b) for c) in d) until e) up f) under g) on

173 to catch a cold; to visit a doctor; to be afflicted by a hereditary disease; to deliver a child; to take a turn for the worse; to perform an autopsy; to remove a tumour; to apply some ointment

174 a) nails, knuckles, palm, wrist b) toe, ankle, calf, knee, thigh c) lips, palate, e(o)sophagus, stomach

175 a) That blow on the head made him feel dizzy.
b) Some natural medicines are made from the bark of trees.
c) One should keep one's first aid kit in a sturdy box.
d) The witch doctor cast an ancient spell on his patient.
e) That is the worst case of the measles I have seen this year.
f) That boy always boxes his little brother when their parents aren't watching.
g) If Mommy blows on that hurt it will feel better.
h) You may take two cases and a handbag on the plane.

i) Could you spell that French word, please?
j) Their dog always barks when cars pass.

Merke:
Worte, die gleich lauten und unterschiedliche Bedeutungen haben, sind Homonyme. Manche Homonyme haben sogar mehr als eine Bedeutung, z.B. das Wort *spell*. Es kann 1. *Zauberspruch*, 2. *buchstabieren* und 3. *Zeitraum* bedeuten.

176 a) mouth b) abdomen of a woman c) mouth d) head e) spine f) abdomen g) face h) nose

177 d) I am sick.

Merke:
Die Sätze a, b, und c bedeuten *Mir ist übel*. *I am sick* heißt dagegen *Ich bin krank*.

178
a) vaccination/inoculation → a method by which the body is made immune to certain diseases
b) indigestion → a condition during which the stomach cannot tolerate certain foods
c) rash → an irritation or inflammation of the skin
d) flatulence → a condition during which gases are produced in the stomach or the intestines
e) a cast → a dressing made with plaster of paris that is applied to broken bones
f) a bruise → a minor injury that causes the skin to change colour temporarily

Merke:
Das Wort *paris* im Begriff *plaster of paris* (deutsch: Gipsverband) kann im Englischen sowohl mit einem großen als auch mit einem kleinen *P* geschrieben werden.

179 a) teeth b) joints c) internal organs

180 a) week b) weak c) heal d) heel e) pain f) panes

181 a) to be hot b) to sweat/perspire c) a malignant tumour d) an endemic disease e) to be of excellent health f) to be corpulent/obese g) to ruin the immune system

182 a) he needed **stitches** b) to apply a **bandage** c) you need **crutches** to walk d) an **adhesive (bandage), Band-Aid (US)** e) pirates wear **eye-patches**

183 toe, ball of the foot, sole, instep or arch, heel, ankle

184 a) a scar b) sunstroke c) Kahlköpfigkeit d) eine Salbe e) to faint f) Schwindelgefühl g) künstliches Gebiß h) to clear one's throat

185 a) epidemic b) allergy c) lethal d) hereditary e) infectious

186
a) A paediatrician is a doctor for children.
b) A dermatologist is a doctor for the skin.
c) A gynaecologist is a doctor for women.
d) An orthopaedist is a doctor for the bones.
e) A dentist is a doctor for the teeth.
f) A psychiatrist is a doctor for the mind.

g) A general practitioner is a doctor for general diseases.
h) A surgeon is a doctor who operates.

187 a) stethoscope b) drill c) blood-pressure apparatus d) X-ray apparatus e) oxygen mask f) syringe g) incubator

188 a) to swallow the pill → in den sauren Apfel beißen
b) to speak one's mind → die Meinung sagen
c) by the skin of one's teeth → mit Hängen und Würgen
d) that gives me the shivers → davon läuft es mir kalt den Rücken runter
e) an eye for an eye, a tooth for a tooth → Auge um Auge, Zahn um Zahn
f) at death's door → dem Tode nahe
g) to be the apple of one's eye → jemandem besonders lieb sein
h) the bone of contention → der Zankapfel
i) to have butterflies in one's stomach → nervös sein
j) by word of mouth → mündlich

Sport and Games / Sport und Spiele

189 a) What kind of sport do you play?
b) When does the match start?
c) What is the score?
d) It's a homegame.
e) She played on our side.
f) The two top teams can still win the competition.
g) Are you a member of a sports club?
h) I engage in sports for recreation only.

190 a) diving b) soccer c) ice skating d) chess e) skiing f) ballroom dancing g) hurdle racing h) boxing i) parachuting, sky diving

191 a) on a football field b) on an athletic field c) on a golf course d) on a tennis court e) on a racing track f) in a swimming-pool g) in a shooting-stand, in a shooting gallery h) in a boxing ring i) in a skating ring j) in the ocean

192 a) a fishing rod b) a golf-club c) boxing gloves d) an épée, a foil e) a hockey stick f) a sledge (UK), sled (US) g) a pair of skis h) a pole i) a cricket bat j) a tennis racket k) a horse l) a bow and arrows m) weights

193 a) hockey match/game b) yacht race c) figure skating competition d) tennis match e) football game f) world championship

194 a) agile, nimble, elegant b) strong, burly c) quick, swift, rapid, fleet d) exact, conscientious e) to accord, to correspond f) delight in, to relish, to like g) to defeat, to crush, to overcome

195 goalkeeper/goalie, the defence, the left back, the right back, the half-back, the left half, the centre half, the right half, the forward

196 d) an instrument for recording humidity

197 a) thoughtless b) unselfish c) unsuccessful d) disobedient e) fearless f) impolite g) imperfect h) unkind i) unfaithful, faithless

Merke:
Antonyme (Gegensätze) werden oft mit den Vorsilben *un-* , *in-* oder *dis-* oder der Nachsilbe *-less* gebildet. Bei Wörtern, die mit den Buchstaben „*m*“ oder „*p*“ anfangen, wird das Antonym statt mit *un-* oder *in-* mit der Vorsilbe *im-* gebildet.

198 a) The game started with the **kick-off** at 2 p.m.
b) The **referee** decided that the goal was not valid.
c) A Russian teenager held the **title** of “World Champion” for two years.
d) At the prize-giving the champion kissed the **cup** she had just won.
e) The **score** of the volleyball match was 4-0.
f) Our ice-hockey team lost because the puck did not enter the **goal** once.

Merke:
Schiedsrichter heißt im Englischen nur im Fußball *referee*. In allen anderen Sportarten heißt es *umpire*.

199 a) Tischtennis b) Dame c) Federball d) Kegeln e) Pfeilwerfen f) Versteckspielen g) Wippen

200 a) players b) die/dice c) shuffle d) board games e) kite f) solution g) magician h) doll house

Merke:
Ein Würfel heißt auf englisch *die*. In der Umgangssprache wird jedoch oft die Mehrzahl *dice* auch als Bezeichnung für nur einen Würfel benutzt.

201 a) hearts → red b) diamonds → red c) spades → black d) clubs → black

202 at a playground

203 a) Please, stay and keep me company b) Nobody kept a straight face c) The coach kept on about d) Always keep your head e) Father kept his word f) keep away from the net g) They kicked him out of the team h) The fans kicked up a fuss

Animals / Tiere

204 a) a bee b) a stork c) a mosquito, a gnat (UK) d) a snake e) a dolphin f) a bat g) a seal h) a giraffe i) a rhinoceros.

205 a) cock/rooster → hen b) drake → duck c) gander → goose d) dog → bitch e) boar → sow f) he-goat → she-goat g) fox → vixen h) lion → lioness

206 Yesterday Dad took the children **to** the zoo. Mom could not join them because she had too much work to do **at/in** her office. There were many animals **at** the zoo. Some were kept **in** cages, others **in** more spacious outside enclosures. The children saw a lazy brown bear that lay **on** her back in the sun all day, while her little cubs climbed **onto/over** her face and her tummy all the time. All they saw of the polar bear were two twinkling eyes, because he hid from the sun **in(side)** a cave. There was much noise in the penguin pen, as those little busybodies constantly jumped **into** their swimming-pool and then climbed **out of** it again.

The children loved the monkeys and Dad had much trouble getting them **away from** the monkey cage. In the evening it was even more difficult to get the children **out of** the zoo and to go home.

Merke:
Es wird unterschieden zwischen Präpositionen, welche eine Richtung angeben (d.h. Bewegung), z.B.: *to, onto, into, (away) from, off, out of,* und solchen, die eine Position bezeichnen, wie *at, on, in* sowie *away from, off* und *out of*.

207 mite, flea, squirrel, eagle, wild boar, rhinoceros, blue whale

208 a) beasts of prey b) Migratory birds c) Amphibians d) mammals e) rodents f) mongrel

209 a) puppy b) kitten c) chick d) lamb e) piglet f) kid g) calf h) (lion) cub i) (bear) cub j) foal/filly

210 a) Die Tiere bitte nicht füttern. b) Vorsicht vor dem Hunde! c) Den Käfig nicht betreten. d) Eintritt verboten.

211 a) A dove → coos. b) A sheep → bleats. c) A wolf → howls. d) A crow → caws. e) A cock → crows. f) A mouse → squeaks. g) A snake → hisses. h) A bee → hums.

212
a) **The swallow** was perched on the cherry tree.
b) **A camel** carried the explorer's luggage across the desert.
c) **The butterfly** flew circles around the rosebush.
d) **A sheep** gives wool for warm pullovers.
e) **A hippopotamus** went for a walk underwater.

213 c) The lions dined on the zebra in only thirty minutes.

Merke:
Eat ist der unfassendste Begriff für *essen*. *Consume* deutet an, daß alles aufgegessen wird, und *devour*, daß viel und schnell gegessen wird. *Feed* bezieht sich nur auf Tiere. *To dine* heißt *eine festliche Mahlzeit einnehmen*.

214 a) dogs → bark and growl b) cats → miaow, meow c) cows → low, moo d) lions → roar and growl e) birds → twitter or sing f) frogs → croak g) nightingales → sing h) ducks → quack

215 a) donkey b) manure c) puppy d) trading e) snail f) wave

Merke:
Worte, die klanglich einem deutschen Wort entsprechen, aber im Englischen eine ganz andere Bedeutung haben, heißen *false friends.* Beim Gebrauch dieser Wörter müssen Sie im besonderen Maße auf die Bedeutung achten.

216 a) den b) nest c) lodge d) hive e) warren f) cobweb g) shell

217 a) pets b) pigeons c) rats d) muzzle e) pedigree f) locusts

218 a) Birds of a feather flock together. b) To kill two birds with one stone. c) It's raining cats and dogs. d) To go to the dogs. e) Every dog has it's day. f) The early bird catches the worm. g) You can't teach an old dog new tricks.

219 a) turtle b) squirrel c) shark d) giraffe e) beetle f) worm

220 d) Karen opened the cages and fled all the animals.

> **Merke:**
> *To set free, to free* und *to release* haben alle die Bedeutung *befreien*. *To flee* heißt *fliehen*. Der grammatisch richtige Satz müßte heißen: *When Karen opened the cages all the animals fled*.

221 a) worker b) actor c) driver d) assistant e) inhabitant f) explorer g) employee h) examiner i) examinee j) examination k) organisation l) imitation

> **Merke:**
> Mit den Nachsilben *-er, -or, -ant, -ee, -ation* sowie *-al, -ment* und *-age* können aus Verben Substantive gebildet werden.

222 a) look b) hear c) meat d) prize e) how f) cabbage

> **Merke:**
> Im Englischen wird zwischen den Worten *flesh* und *meat*, beide bedeuten im Deutschen *Fleisch*, unterschieden. *Flesh* bezieht sich in der Regel auf menschliches Fleisch oder Fruchtfleisch, während *meat* für tierisches Fleisch benutzt wird.

223 d) a needle used to fasten separate articles together

224 a) trunk → the long, tubelike muscle that elephants use for sucking
b) prey → an animal that is caught by another for food
c) fangs → the long, sharp teeth that animals use to tear prey
d) scales → the many small flat plates that cover a fish's body
e) bill → the mouth of a bird
f) shell → the hard, rigid cover of a tortoise's body

225 a) Er ist mausetot. b) Den Brunnen zudecken, wenn das Kind ertrunken ist. c) Ganz aus dem Häuschen sein. d) Sich köstlich amüsieren. e) Sich wie ein Elefant im Porzellanladen benehmen. f) Übergeschnappt sein.

226 b) the larva of a butterfly or a moth
d) the name of a tractor that moves on two steel belts and not on wheels

227 a) a herd of elephants b) a swarm of bees c) a pack of wolves d) a school of dolphins e) a flight of birds f) a family of lions

Plants / Pflanzen

228 a) in b) on c) with d) by e) to f) of

229 a) daisy → Gänseblümchen b) cornflower → Kornblume c) daffodil → Narzisse d) dandelion → Löwenzahn e) lily of the valley → Maiglöckchen f) carnation → Nelke g) forget-me-not → Vergißmeinnicht

230 a) cherry blossoms b) Crocus blooms c) seeds of a dandelion d) grains of wheat e) buds

Merke:
Die Blüten eines Baumes heißen auf englisch *blossoms*, die Blüten von Bumen jedoch *blooms.* Der allgemeine Begriff für Samen ist *seed*, ein Getreidekorn heißt aber auch *grain*.

231
a) core and kernel → Gehäuse und Kern
b) husk and chaff → Hülse und Spreu
c) trunk and branch → Stamm und Ast
d) stalk and peel → Stiel und Schale
e) stump and log → Stumpf und gefällter Baumstamm

232 a) shell b) peel c) skin d) petal

233 b) The shape of these flowers reminds me of my grandmother's garden.

Merke:
Die Worte *smell, scent, fragrance* und *perfume* verweisen auf einen *Geruch*. Das Wort *shape* heißt auf deutsch *äußere Form*.

234
a) vegetable plant → a plant grown for a part that will be eaten
b) ornamental shrub → a bush grown for its beauty
c) coniferous tree → evergreen trees that have cones
d) bulbs → the swollen, round part of plants (such as tulips) that is underground
e) edible mushrooms → a small, fleshy plant with a stem and a cap
f) deciduous trees → trees that loose their leaves in winter

235 c) a fast-growing plant of no value

236 People love to be surprised with a **bunch** of flowers. The **scent** of some flowers can fill an entire room with a pleasant smell. Unfortunately, there is only little time to **admire** the beauty of cut flowers, because they lose their freshness and **fade** after a few days.

237

s	t	v	i	o	l	e	t	a	r	g
p	e	o	n	y	o	k	u	b	s	e
o	r	g	e	d	u	n	l	a	b	n
d	g	i	r	i	s	u	i	e	e	t
a	u	r	m	e	l	l	p	s	a	i
i	n	u	d	r	e	s	t	a	n	a
s	u	n	f	l	o	w	e	r	y	n
y	n	o	t	h	e	s	r	e	g	u
p	l	b	l	u	e	b	e	l	l	e
a	s	e	p	h	o	n	e	m	e	n
w	o	e	d	e	l	w	e	i	s	s

238 a) cabbage b) buttercup c) bamboo d) rice

239 a) mistletoe b) ebony c) bark d) needles e) foliage f) vine g) Toadstools

240 a) rosebud b) pine cone c) blueberry d) sunflower e) beetroot f) mushroom g) coffee bean

241 a) to **protect** nature b) to **perform** genetic manipulation c) to **maintain** the ecological balance d) **produce** acid rain e) **increase** the size of the ozone hole

242 a) ugly, unpleasant, terrible b) stench, odour, stink c) barren, unfruitful, desolate, infertile d) colourless, drab, dull e) above ground, visible f) smooth, regular, even

Travelling and Transportation / Reise und Verkehr

243 a) station b) airport c) harbour, port d) bus station e) parking lot f) bicycle stand

244 a) a **one-way** or a return ticket b) a **window** or an aisle seat c) the smoking or the **non-smoking** section d) first or **second** class

245 a) much is b) leave c) exchange d) arrive e) check f) travelling

246 a) Is this seat free? b) May I open the window? c) Please, fill in these forms. d) Children under six are free of charge. e) May I see your ticket, please? f) Have a pleasant journey!

247 a) platform → the area from which you enter a train
b) destination → the place at the end of a journey
c) aisle → a passage between sections of seats
d) couchette → a train compartment with six narrow beds
e) supplement → an additional price for special trains, ships etc.
f) reduced rate → a cheaper price for children, students, etc.
g) souvenir → something bought to remind one of a journey

Merke:
Schlafwagen heißt auf englisch *sleeper* oder *sleeping compartment*, *ein Liegewagen* ist auf englisch *a couchette*.

248 a) waiting room b) departure c) arrival d) customs e) duty-free f) left-luggage g) emergency

249 a) travel agency, tourist office b) aeroplane, plane c) bus or train d) train e) ship or an aeroplane f) ship g) ship

Merke:
Für *Flugzeug* gibt es im Englischen drei gleichwertige Wörter: das ursprüngliche Wort *aeroplane*, der besonders in Amerika gängige Begriff *airplane* und die Abkürzung *plane*.

250 a) **monthly** ticket b) sleeping **compartment** c) ferry d) **freight/goods** trains e) schedule

251 a) ein Verkehrsflugzeug

252 a) Take b) boarding c) goes d) bus stop e) get off

253 a) double room b) room key c) continental breakfast d) wake-up call e) room service f) porter g) swimming pool

254 a) got on his nerves b) get round c) get along well d) get a word in e) get out of bed f) get over with g) get through

Merke:
Das Wort *Ferien* heißt im amerikanischen Englisch *vacation*, im britischen Englisch aber *holiday*. Im Amerikanischen wird *holiday* für *Feiertag* gebraucht.

255 a) a smuggler b) a passenger c) a guest d) a tour-guide e) a stowaway f) a tourist

256 a) for b) in c) with d) by e) of/for f) with

Merke:
*To arrive **in** Charlotte* bedeutet *in der Stadt Charlotte ankommen*. Möchten Sie aber darauf hinweisen, daß Sie an einem Flughafen ankommen, so verwenden Sie die Präposition **at**: *to arrive **at** Charlotte Airport*. *What is wrong with you?* heißt *Was ist los mit Dir?* und **nicht** *Was ist falsch?*

257 c) the situation when too many cars block the street

258 a) tracks b) engine c) compartments d) conductor e) berths

259 a) barge → Lastkahn b) sailing-ship → Segelschiff c) wreck → Wrack d) life-boat → Rettungsboot e) raft → Floß f) steamer → Dampfer g) trawler → Fischdampfer mit Schleppnetz h) tug(boat) → Schlepper

260 a) lighthouse b) buoys c) oars d) quay e) portholes f) gangway

261 a) to launch a ship b) to put to sea c) to call at a port d) to go ashore e) to embark f) to capsize

262 a) the runway b) the propellers c) a balloon d) glider e) the cockpit f) the jet engines g) a helicopter

263 b) eine Strecke hinter sich bringen

264 a) a truck (US), a lorry (UK) b) a motorcycle, a motorbike c) a side-car d) a (motor-) car, an automobile (US) e) a caravan

265 a) the brake b) the horn, the hooter (UK) c) the mudguard (US), the fender (UK) d) the clutch e) the licence plate (US), the number-plate (UK) f) the indicator g) the tire, tyre (UK) h) the (fuel) tank

266 b) the panel that holds the steering wheel and the controls

267 a) to change the gear b) the car broke down c) to jack up a car d) to change a tire e) to check the ignition f) to lubricate a ball-bearing

268 d) Don't underestimate the hostilities of a German highway!

Merke:
Danger bezieht sich sowohl auf große als auch auf kleine Gefahren. *Peril* und *threat* warnen vor äußerst großen Gefahren, und *hazards* bezieht sich auf solche Gefahren, die eine Aktion noch risikoreicher machen. *Hostilities* heißt hingegen *Feindseligkeiten*. Grammatisch richtig wäre *Don't underestimate the hostilities* ***on*** *a German highway!*

269 a) accelerator → Gaspedal b) fuel consumption → Brennstoffverbrauch c) headlight → Scheinwerfer d) bonnet → Haube e) radiator → Kühler f) boot → Kofferraum

Merke:
Viele Autoteile haben im amerikanischen und im britischen Englisch verschiedene Namen, z.B. trunk (US) → boot (UK), fender (UK) → mudguard (US), gas (US) → petrol (UK).

270 a) to break the news to somebody b) to drive a wedge between them c) to achieve a break-through d) to drive someone crazy e) you know what I'm driving at f) to break away from something g) to break new ground h) to drive something home to somebody

271
a) Q: I'd like a ticket to Freiburg, please. A: One-way or return?
b) Q: Is this seat taken? A: No, it's free.
c) Q: I would like a room for one night, please. A: Would you like it with or without bathroom?
d) Q: Is this the right bus to the theatre? A: No, you are going in the wrong direction.
e) Q: Could you take me to Harvey Street quickly? A: Certainly, we will be there in about ten minutes.

Other Places / Andere Orte

272 a) capital b) ocean c) continent d) mountain range e) island f) river g) natives

273 b) Einwohner/in

274 a) Poland → a Pole b) Canada → a Canadian c) Germany → a German d) Belgium → a Belgian e) France → a Frenchman, a Frenchwoman f) The United States of America → an (U.S.) American g) India → an Indian h) The Philippines → a Filipino, a Filipina i) Scotland → a Scot, a Scotsman, a Scotswoman j) New Zealand → a New Zealander k) The Czech Republic → a Czech l) Greece → a Greek

275 a) a Mexican → Mexico b) a Dutchwoman → The Netherlands c) an Egyptian → Egypt d) a Spaniard → Spain e) a Hungarian → Hungary f) an Italian → Italy g) an Irishman → Ireland h) a Thai → Thailand i) a Turk → Turkey j) a Japanese → Japan k) a Portuguese → Portugal

Merke:
Der Name für die Bewohner und Bewohnerinnen eines Landes wird immer groß geschrieben und immer mit dem Artikel benutzt, z.B.: *I am **a** Kenyan* oder *Randall is **the** American of the group*.

276 a) Italian b) French c) Indian d) African e) German f) Chinese g) Swiss h) Russian i) Scottish

277 north, south, east, west

278 a) smaller b) biggest c) colder d) older e) highest f) driest

Merke:
Einsilbige Adjektive sowie zweisilbige Adjektive, die auf *-y, -le* oder *-ow* enden, werden durch das Anhängen der Nachsilben *-er* und *-est* an das Grundwort gesteigert. Manchmal ändert sich stattdessen das ganze Wort.

279 a) rainforest b) landscape c) hillside d) high tide e) sunrise f) earthquake g) seashore h) South Pole

280 a) a spring → a place where water comes out of the ground b) a moor → a very wet area of wasteland c) a volcano → a mountain that issues smoke and fire d) a beach → the place where the land meets the sea e) a tributary → a river that joins a bigger river or a lake f) a peak → the highest point on a mountain

281 a) most interesting b) most beautiful c) more boring d) more humid e) more difficult f) most nervous g) more frightened

Merke:
Drei- und mehrsilbige Adjektive werden mit Hilfe der Wörter *more* und *most* gesteigert.

282 a) Turkish b) Portuguese c) Norwegian d) Finnish e) Swedish f) English g) French h) Hungarian i) Danish j) Greek k) Icelandic l) Kashmiri m) Persian n) Catalan o) Slovene

283 a) saw the beautiful scenery b) famous national monument c) height of the tides d) ruin of the destroyed church e) photo-safari went through six African countries f) inside the game reserve

284 a) pebble, stone, rock, hill, mountain b) brook, rivulet, river c) pond, lake, sea, ocean d) breeze, wind, gale, storm, hurricane

285 a) gentle, gradual b) wide, vast, spacious c) deep d) low e) short, brief, small f) safe, harmless

286 a) The skyline of New York City moves from year to year.

Merke:
Change und *alter* können jede Art der Veränderung bezeichnen. *Transform* bezeichnet grundlegende Veränderungen, *modify* jedoch nur kleine. *Move* bedeutet *bewegen*: es ist hier falsch.

287 a) height b) to check c) valuable d) to scream

288 a) helpful friend b) useless car c) sleepy dog d) readable book e) countable number

History and Politics/ Geschichte und Politik

289 a) tyrant b) refugee c) legislator d) diplomat e) conspirator f) revolutionary g) rebel h) representative i) voter

290 a) government b) cabinet c) prime minister, Premier d) chancellor e) an election f) ministry g) a party

291 a) down the ages b) at various times c) a sign of the times d) To the best of my memory e) in our times

292 a) overthrow b) entered c) called d) discussed e) formed f) adjourned g) held

293 b) This is the first time a woman was appointed as Minister of Defence.

Merke:
Einfacher wäre *This is the first time a woman was made Minister of Defence*.

294 a) to contradict → to resist somebody in an argument b) to conspire → to secretly plan an unlawful act c) to condemn → to declare that something is wrong and punishable d) constituency → a group of citizens allowed to elect a representative e) conviction → a strong belief

295 b) She did not share his views on politics. d) She did not share his opinion on politics.

Merke:
Eine Meinung haben heißt auf englisch *to have an opinion* oder *to have views on something*. *Meaning* heißt *Bedeutung*, und *sight* heißt *die Aussicht*.

296 a) **Head** of Government b) **Municipal** Officer c) **Deputy** President d) Ministry of **Commerce** e) Secretary of **State** f) Ministry of **Internal Affairs**

297 a) to levy taxes b) to adopt a resolution c) to mount the throne d) to crush an uprising e) to confer a medal f) to elect to an office g) to cast a vote

298 c) the process of uniting two or more groups

299 a) ballot b) nobility c) subjects d) sovereign e) realm

300 a) society b) salary c) appoint

301 c) to sue

302 a) Middle Ages b) Renaissance c) modern times d) Stone Age

303 a) conclusion b) weakness c) meeting d) security

304 a) weak, feeble, powerless b) antisocial, asocial, misanthropic c) irresponsible, unstable d) unkind, callous, cruel, cold-blooded

305 b) a process by which one seeks justice in a court

306 a) goodness b) length c) government d) width e) continuation

Merke:
Viele Hauptwörter werden durch das Anhängen von Nachsilben wie *-er*, *-tion*, *-acy*, *-ness* oder *-ment* an ein Verb oder Adjektiv gebildet.

307 a) countries b) attend c) society d) won

308 a) limit b) frontier c) border d) limit

Merke:
Limit bezeichnet eine Grenze, die nicht überschritten werden darf. Dagegen verweisen *border* und *frontier* auf landschaftliche Grenzen, in der Regel Staatsgrenzen. *Frontier* kann auch die Grenze eines besiedelten Gebiets bedeuten.

309 c) a professional historian

The Arts / Die Schönen Künste

310 a) piano b) organ c) bagpipes d) guitar e) bugle f) cymbals g) harps

311 a) Q: What **kind/type of music** do you like? b) Q: Do you **play an instrument**?

312 a) favourite b) tuned up c) accompanied d) venues

313 a) encore b) the strings c) to audition d) chamber music e) the scale f) major g) minor

314 After one month of intense rehearsing, the orchestra was ready to give a **performance**. They played an unusually modern **interpretation** of Beethoven's Ninth Symphony.
The audience was delighted by it and gave a standing **ovation**. When the soloists **took their bows** many listeners threw flowers on the stage.

315 a) a singer b) a drummer c) a violinist d) a conductor

316 a) insensitive b) inexperienced c) careless d) ungenerous

Merke:
Das englische Wort *sensitive* bedeutet auf deutsch *sensibel.* Das englische Wort *sensible* aber heißt auf deutsch *vernünftig*.

317 b) a wind instrument made of wood with 8 finger holes

318 a) grand piano b) castanets c) banjo d) strings e) saxophone

319

d	e	a	f	e	n	**h**	o	o	p	s
r	e	s	t	**p**	**i**	**a**	**n**	**o**	e	l
u	t	r	a	n	n	**r**	u	g	m	**b**
m	s	**t**	**r**	**u**	**m**	**p**	**e**	**t**	j	**a**
s	d	o	c	k	s	**s**	g	i	t	**n**
e	e	**v**	**i**	**o**	**l**	**i**	**n**	l	e	**j**
p	e	t	t	y	s	**c**	**e**	**l**	**l**	**o**
h	s	o	t	m	p	**h**	n	r	u	f
e	**o**	p	i	e	f	**o**	o	u	y	e
j	e	**r**	**c**	**l**	**a**	**r**	**i**	**n**	**e**	**t**
d	o	n	**n**	i	k	**d**	g	o	o	m

320 e) the thumb hole of a wind instrument

321 a) thyme b) combine c) choir d) rough

322 a) by b) after c) to d) in e) on

323 a) to sight-read music → Musik vom Blatt spielen b) to tune an instrument → ein Instrument stimmen c) to be flat → zu tief sein d) to be out of tune → verstimmt sein e) to play by heart → auswendig spielen f) to give the keynote → den Grundton angeben

324 a) eine untergeordnete Rolle spielen b) für fast gar nichts c) viel Aufhebens um etwas machen d) den Umständen entsprechend handeln

325 b) a very long prose story

326 c) I need a copy of the Riverside Shakespeare.

327 a) ein Gedicht b) eine Zeile c) ein Absatz d) ein Kapitel e) ein Band

328 a) diary b) review c) play d) non-fiction e) Nursery rhymes

329 a) a summary of the plot → eine Zusammenfassung der Handlung
b) an abridged encyclop(a)edia → ein gekürztes Lexikon
c) the gist of the talk was clear → die Hauptaussage war deutlich
d) engravings illustrated the poems → Stiche stellten die Gedichte dar

330 a) a painter b) a sculptor/sculptress c) a composer d) a poet/poetess

331 a) box-office b) cloak room c) playbill d) part/role

332 a) put words into my mouth b) putting on c) put his foot into it d) put my finger on it

333 c) die großen Handlungsabschnitte